MW01116023

Meet
With God

ANY TIME
ANY PLACE

JENNIE J. CHAPMAN

FOREWORD BY PASTOR SCOTT ADAMS

Author photo by Lani Evans Adams

Cover Photo by Bobby R Chapman, Jr

Edited by Lani Evans Adams & Tammy Gathings

Formatted by Jen Henderson at Wild Words Formatting

Cover Graphics Coordinated by Angie Alaya at Fiverr

Table of Contents

Foreword

Dear Reader,

If you desire a more intimate relationship with God, then the book you hold in your hands is a road map for that very destination. I have been a pastor for nearly 27 years and the one thing that I am sure of is that there are depths in God that have not been fully explored, much less obtained. The Apostle Paul in his letter to the Ephesian Church, prayed that they would come to know, not only the height, but also the depth of God. My observation is that many Christians are satisfied with a surface level relationship with Christ.

Your acquisition of this book indicates that you desire more! We must realize that it is not only God's will that all men be saved but also that once saved they continue until they come to a knowledge of the Truth. After having the author of this book attend the church I pastor since 2008, I can assure you that the steps she outlines in this book have been part of her walk with God for many years.

Meeting with God should be as natural to a believer as a child's desire to sit in their father's lap and the steps laid out in *Meet with God* are arranged in the optimal order for that to happen. As an adamant student and teacher of the God's Word, I am grateful that the very first chapter places emphasis on the Word of God. This is vital, not only in our intimate times with Him, but also for our Christian walk as well.

As Jennie encourages and cautions in the book, do not skip ahead! This book and the steps are to be a lifestyle not a quick fix or a simple formula. So take your time reading, begin to put it into practice and you'll begin to see your relationship with The Savior intensify and grow more intimate. Remember, intimacy with your Heavenly Father is a natural desire for His children and His Word is the bedrock for all our interactions with Him.

—Pastor Scott Adams
The Living Word Ministries and Outreach, Inc.
Chesterfield, South Carolina

Preface

Thus says the Lord, the God of Israel: Write all the words that I have spoken to you in a book.

Jeremiah 30:2 AMPC

Once again, here we are with another book inspired by Holy Spirit. In saying this, let it be known that our **Heavenly Father**, **Jesus**, and **Holy Spirit** are the **true Authors** of this book. As with four of my other books listed below:

> *"Encounters with Him: Knowing that Still Small Voice"*
>
> *"Overcomers by Faith Devotional/Journal: 100 Days of Seeking His Face"*
>
> *"8 Steps to a New Beginning: Building Relationship with the Holy Trinity"*
>
> *"Simplicity in Hearing God Speak: Led by His Voice"*

The book you hold in your hand, along with those listed were actually downloaded to me. If you received a copy of those previously listed books, you'll find the story of how each one came into being a book. You can also go to my author website, (*https://www.JennieJChapman.com*) to read about each, and there are excerpts from each listed there. Please feel free to also leave a *Review*. It is really supernatural how the Trinity has orchestrated each book in such dynamic ways. I love how Holy Spirit moves on me as I give myself to Him and what He wants to say.

Let me tell you the story of this book. The title actually came to me in January 2013, while my pastor was preaching/teaching. I literally heard him say, "*Meet with God.*" Those words pierced my spirit-man. I couldn't wait to find out where he got that from, however, when I asked Him, he didn't remember saying those words at all. So, I got the CD of that service and listened and listened, but my pastor had not said those words! This led me on a study to see where, or if these very words where even in the Bible. To my surprise, though I had read the Bible through many times, these exact words where right there in black and white. We find them in Exodus 19:17…

> *And Moses brought the people out of the camp to* ***meet with God****, and they stood at the foot of the mountain.*

When we read this story, God had asked Moses to have the people of Israel to prepare themselves to meet with

Him. There were stipulations, which the Israelites at first, agreed to, however, in the end they couldn't follow His commands. To *Meet with God,* we must obey His commands as to how to enter into His Presence. Entering into His Presence is what I received from hearing those words, *Meet with God.* I pursued Him and His very Presence till I was consumed with meeting with my God. Then in 2016, I was led to have a prayer meeting where we had no agenda, no personal request, no time limit, and we were only there to *Meet with God.* These meetings were so powerful, as we were there to only minister to Him. In doing so, He would usually speak to us as a congregation, and to this little prayer group's hunger for His Presence. He entered into our sanctuary with His very Glory that was seen once in the natural, and many times in pictures. When He would show up in His Glory, He would lead one of the prayers to take a picture, and there He was manifested in those pictures! He not only showed us His Glory, but He healed bodies, and answered the secret petitions of our hearts. We were not seeking these things, only His face, therefore He blessed us for setting aside an *unlimited* amount of time just to minister to Him. We did not leave until we sensed He was fully ministered to.

On with how this book came into being. In 2024, a friend and I were discussing God's Presence, and how people just do not know how to enter into His Presence. She stated that we need to have a *Meet with God* meeting, as she said those words, Holy Spirit quickened me, and

I just *knew at that moment* that He had another book to teach on how to enter His Presence, and the title was *Meet with God*. Thus, that's how this book began. He then started giving me chapters and verses. And here we are with book number five, written by the Holy Trinity.

As you read this book, I do pray for a deeper understanding of how to *Meet with God*. Your relationship with *Father God, Jesus,* and *Holy Spirit* is key to entering into His Presence. It's not about religion, but RELATIONSHIP. Let's prepare to enter into His Presence!

Make a joyful shout to the LORD, all you lands!
Serve the LORD with gladness;
come before His presence with singing.
Know that the LORD, He is God;
it is He who has made us, and not we ourselves;
we are His people and the sheep of His pasture.
Enter into His gates with thanksgiving,
and into His courts with praise.
Be thankful to Him, and bless His name.
For the LORD is good; His mercy is everlasting,
and His truth endures to all generations.

Psalm 100

Introduction

God longs for us to come before Him (Heb 4:16) and meet with Him at any moment of any day. This is a Bible promise for us, if we have accepted Jesus as Lord of our life. If you have not accepted Jesus, we will address that later in this section. For now and as in my other books, I must give you a full disclaimer once more. As I have previously stated, **the true Authors** are actually, our **Heavenly Father, Jesus,** and **Holy Spirit**. They have chosen to use me as their earthen vessel (Jer 30:2), as an instrument for Their glory. For such, I am truly overwhelmingly humbled. With our God being glorified in this book, please note that the name *satan* and all names related to him are **not** capitalized, for he is the little god (2 Cor 4:4) of this world. I reserved my right to not capitalize his name, even though by doing so, I am violating grammar rules.

As you read this book, you will learn ways to prepare yourself to *Meet with God*. You will begin to know that it is His will for you to come boldly before Him. He wants to meet with you even more than you want to meet with Him. He created man to fellowship with Him. If we follow His commands, we will enter right into His courts. As we build relationship, we will see that we are actually walking together (2Cor 6:16). If we belong to Him then He lives on the inside of us and we have total access to Him, and Him to us!

As stated at the beginning of this introduction, let's take care of first things first. If you have not accepted Jesus into your heart and asked Him to come in and abide with you, please do so now. Jesus said, *"My sheep hear My voice, and I know them, and they follow Me"* (John 10:27). If we have not given our whole heart to Him, then how can we expect to hear Him speak?

I will lead you in a prayer of repentance and acceptance of all Jesus has for you. We will pray according to Romans 10:9-10:

> … that if you confess with your mouth the Lord Jesus and believe in your heart that God has raised Him from the dead, you will be saved. For with the heart one believes unto righteousness, and with the mouth confession is made unto salvation.

Please read the prayer below and mean it with all your heart, and afterwards be sure to tell someone that you gave your heart to Jesus. You can bless me with that testimony by going to my author's website (*https://www.jenniejchapman.com*) and clicking on '*Contact.*'

INTRODUCTION

Let's pray:

> Father God, I thank You for the giving of Your Son (Isa 53:4-5), so that He could live, die, and be raised (Acts 10:40), so that I might have eternal life (Rom 6:23). I now receive His sacrifice on my behalf. I repent of all my sins, and ask Jesus to be Lord of my life. I thank You that His blood has atoned for my sin. Now I am clean, as white as snow (1John 1:9). I thank You that Jesus will baptize me with Holy Spirit and fire (Matt 3:11), that I may be Your disciple all the days of my life. Thank You Father God. In Jesus' name. Amen.

Chapter 1
THE WORD

---

*… that He might sanctify and cleanse her
with the washing of water by the word…*

Ephesians 5:26

When we read the verses that surround the above verse
we find that Jesus is telling husbands to love their wives,
just as He also loved the church and gave Himself for
her, that He might sanctify and cleanse her with the
washing of water by the word, that He might present her to
Himself a glorious church, not having spot or wrinkle or
any such thing, but that she should be *holy and without
blemish* (Eph 5:25-27). The washing of water by the word
is simply to be washed by the cleansing power of God's
Word. As we read the Holy Scriptures, they begin to
wash us, and cleanse us, so that we become holy and

without blemish. This speaks of the church body, and pertains to each of us individually, as we are His body and members in particular (1Cor 12:27). The Word changes us into His image from glory to glory (2Cor 3:18). The more we read His *Word*, the more it washes us, and our thought process begins to change (Phil 4:8).

Heavenly Father has placed in each of us, a heart to know Him (Jer 24:7). When we seek Him out, we will actually fall in love with the God of His *Word*. There will be a hunger to really *know* Him (John 10:14). How do we grow in the knowledge of Him? When we seek Him with our whole heart (Jer 29:13), by reading His *Word*, praying, and fasting. He promises we will find Him! Let's look at Jeremiah 29:11-14:

> For I know the thoughts that I think toward you, says the LORD, thoughts of peace and not of evil, to give you a future and a hope. Then you will call upon Me and go and pray to Me, and I will listen to you. And you will seek Me and find Me, when you search for Me with all your heart. I will be found by you, says the LORD…

That word *seek* {H1245} in the Strong's Concordance actually carries the meaning to seek to *find*, to seek to *secure*, to *seek the face*, to *desire*, demand, to require, exact, to ask, request. WOW! That's how He wants us to seek Him. If we simply seek His face, we will simply find Him. When I say, "Seek His face," I don't mean we are looking to find His face, but rather we use our God given imagination and see Him in our mind. As we gaze upon Him with our mind's screen, we are saying to Him, "I am here Lord, just You and me." Let's take a look at a verse that will explain this better. We find it in Psalm 27:4 AMPC:

> One thing have I asked of the Lord,
> that will I *seek*, *inquire* for, and [*insistently*] require:
> that I may *dwell* in the house of the Lord
> [in His presence] *all the days of my life*,
> to *behold and gaze* upon the beauty [the sweet attractiveness and the delightful loveliness] of the Lord and
> to *meditate*, *consider*, and *inquire* in His temple.

From this we can see the importance of knowing the Word. This one verse, where David was still alive, shows us that we can go from the earth to the heavenlies at any given moment. If we're focused primarily on the earth, we'll act as a mere man, BUT if we primarily focus our eyes on the heavenly realm, we'll act accordingly! Our spirit-man will be alive unto God in Christ Jesus (Rom 6:11), and able to see into the heavenly realm at any given moment, that is, if we are invited, as Daniel and John *saw* into the heavens. Let's look at those verses:

> Daniel 7:13:
> I was watching in the night visions,
> and behold, *One* like the Son of Man,
> coming with the clouds of heaven!

13

He came to the Ancient of Days,
and they brought Him near before Him.

Revelation 4:4
'John sees the Throne Room of Heaven'
After these things I looked, and behold, a door standing open in heaven. And the first voice which I heard was like a trumpet speaking with me, saying, "Come up here, and I will show you things which must take place after this."

Both Daniel and John knew the Holy Scriptures. They were students of the Word of God, as we must also be (2Tim 2:15). Both Daniel and John loved God with their whole heart. They actually had relationship with the God of the universe. It's impossible to imagine seeing God or Jesus without loving them both. We have all read or at least heard where God had said, "Thou canst not see My face: for there shall no man see Me, and live (Ex 33:20)." When I read this verse, I think of how we must *die* to self (Rom 8:13), if we want to commune with the Holy Trinity. If we do a cross reference of where we read God saying this (Ex 33:20), we find that others have seen God and lived. For example in Genesis 32:30 Jacob stated that he had seen God face to face, and his life was preserved. Then in Exodus 24:9-10 we read where Moses, Aaron, Nadab, Abihu, and seventy of the elders of Israel actually saw the God of Israel, and lived also. Our sin is what separates us from God. But, when we truly love Him, we will want to be stripped of all our fleshly ways. We have read and heard time and time again where the Gospels state that John was the disciple whom Jesus loved. In fact, the AMPC version states that Jesus *esteemed* and *delighted* in John, as John was leaning on His bosom. WOW, how much more will He do the same for us as we lean upon Him! Let's look at this verse in John 13:23:

> Now there was leaning on Jesus' bosom *one* of His disciples, *whom Jesus loved.*

Note that this does not say that John was *the only one* Jesus loved! Read it again. It says that there was leaning on Jesus' bosom <u>*one of His disciples*</u>, *whom Jesus loved*. See how important it is to study the Word of God? The more we study, the more we learn, the more the verses speak to us individually. Just this verse alone adds us to the list of those whom Jesus loved, esteemed, and delighted in. All because we are His disciples! Glory!

When we love someone, we imagine ourselves with them, and make plans to meet together. We don't want that time to fade, but rather last as long as possible. How much more does our Heavenly Father also want to meet with us on an unlimited schedule? Let's look at another verse that will help us to use our imagination to enter into the Heavenly realm. We find this verse in Isaiah 26:3:

> You will keep him in perfect peace, whose mind is stayed on You, because he trusts in You.

That word *mind* {H3336} carries the meaning of *imagination*. So we could say, "He will keep us in perfect peace, as we *gaze intently* with our *imagination* upon Him!" WOW! There we go, Biblical text as how to keep our mind on Him with our imagination. We all have an image of God and Jesus that we *see* when we think on Them. However you see Them is the way you will connect. Let's look at what David said in Psalm 16:8:

> I have set the LORD always before me: because He is at my right hand, I shall not be moved.

David is saying that he had *set* the LORD *ever* before himself. We too need to begin to train ourselves to walk constantly aware of His Presence. We can read in 2Corinthians 6:16 (KJV) that God actually walks in us. I love that. He is the one who sticks closer than a brother, in fact, let's take a look at that verse in Proverbs 18:24:

> A man *who has* friends must himself be friendly, but there is a friend *who* sticks closer than a brother.

When we search out the word *friend* {H157}, we find that it means to have affection for; to be love (-d, -ly). The beginning of the verse states that in order to have a friend we must first show ourselves friendly. How much more do we need to show ourselves friendly, and in love with Jesus? I have heard it said that, "Only what you are aware of, is natural to you." Think about it, what you *see* is what you are aware of. You see this book, you see the words, you see the things around you, and thus you are aware of them. My hope is that by the end of this book, you will have learned to see Jesus, and be *aware* of His Presence, constantly with you. So much that it becomes natural to you, or as people like to say, "That it becomes second nature." If we can get to that point, we will have what we need, because we'd have grown in-love with Him to the point that we know He is in us and we are in Him! Let's look at a popular verse. It's 1 John 4:4:

> *You are of God,* little children, and have overcome them, because **He who is in you** is greater than he who is in the world.

We also know that when we asked Jesus to be LORD of our life, He came to live on the inside of us, and sent Holy Spirit to be in us. In fact, that verse states that the world *cannot see* Him! Let's look at that in John 14:15-31:

Jesus Promises Another Helper:

> "If you love Me, keep My commandments. And I will pray the Father, and He will give you another Helper, that He may abide with you forever— the Spirit of truth, *whom the world **cannot** receive*, because it **neither sees** Him nor **knows** Him; but you know Him, for He dwells *with* you and will be *in* you. I will not leave you orphans; I will come to you.

We just read where the world cannot receive Him, nor even can *see* Him! When we search out that word *see* {G2334}, we find that it carries the meaning of; to look at, to behold, to view attentively, to *view mentally,* consider, to *perceive with the eyes*, to *enjoy the presence of* one, to discern, and to *find out by seeing*! God's eyes are ever on us, in fact 2Chronicles 16:9 we find that the eyes of the Lord run to and fro throughout the whole earth to show Himself strong in behalf of those whose hearts are blameless toward Him. He created us to commune with Him, that's not in the by and by, or when we get to Heaven. He means in our everyday, ordinary, rising up, and laying down life. He even meets with us in our dreams. He is always watching and waiting for us to come near to Him.

In this chapter, hopefully we can see where knowing the Word of God is vital to having a relationship with the Trinity. We must not only read, but study (2Tim 2:15), because to know what a particular word actually means, is vital. The more we read and learn the Word, the more we will fall in love with the Creator of the universe. The more we love Him, the more we want to be with Him. Loving Him is key to entering into a *meeting with Him*. But if we do not acknowledge that we are aware that He is in us and with us, then why should He manifest Himself to us? It's in the love for Him that causes us to long to be with Him. The Word tells us that an earthly father knows how to be good to his children, so how much more does our Heavenly Father? Let's look at those verses in Matthew 7:9-11:

> Or what man is there among you who, if his son asks for bread, will give him a stone? Or if he asks

for a fish, will he give him a serpent? If you then, being evil, know how to give good gifts to your children, how much more will your Father who is in heaven give good things to those who ask Him!

How much more will our Heavenly Father bless us with His Presence? I sense the need to explain our access in experiencing the Holy Trinity. First our Heavenly Father is God (Isa 45:5), and we have access to Him through the shed blood of Jesus (John 14:6) that we accepted when we asked Him to be LORD of our life. Jesus shed that blood for us, died, and rose again promising us that God would send Holy Spirit (John 14:26), so that we would not be alone and without help. We only have access to the Father through the Son, and Father God sent Holy Spirit in Jesus' name to lead us in all truth (John 16:13). We already read where the Word stated that the world would not recognize Holy Spirit, because they can't *see* Him! Let's look at that particular verse once again in John 14:17 AMPC:

> The Spirit of Truth, Whom the world cannot receive (welcome, take to its heart), because it *does not see* Him or *know* and *recognize* Him. But you know *and* recognize Him, for He lives with you [*constantly*] and will be in you.

We need to meditate on this verse. It is telling us to *know* and *recognize* Him. That word *know* {G1097} carries with it the meanings of to learn, to know, come to know, get a knowledge of, perceive, to understand, to be intimate

19

with—as a husband and wife are, and to become acquainted with. If we really want to *Meet with God*, we have got to learn to be intimate with Him. We can't be intimate if we can't *see* or *imagine* Him. Here's one more verse that explains that it is Biblical to come before Him, and to His throne. We find that in Hebrews 4:16:

> Let us therefore *come* **boldly** *to the throne* of grace, that we may obtain mercy and find grace to help in time of need.

As this chapter comes to a close, prayerfully you are encouraged to learn more of the Word of God which will cause us to know more of Him, and fall deeper and deeper in love with Him. The Word of God is always our guideline to encountering the Trinity. The Word we know will cause us to know Him more which in turn will show us more ways of entering into His throne and courts. If we know His *Word*, then we know Him. John 1:14 states, "And the Word was made flesh, and dwelt among us, (and we *beheld* His glory, the glory as of the only begotten of the Father,) full of grace and truth." May we see Him as He is, and thus so shall we be (2Cor 3:18).

Let me pray for you:

> Heavenly Father, thank You for sending Jesus to die for us, and thank You Jesus for preparing the way for Holy Spirit to be with us. We acknowledge that You and Your Word are the same (John 1:14).

Now Father, I ask You to continue to give wisdom, knowledge, and understanding to all those who have read this chapter (Pro 2:6). May they begin to read Your Word and receive all that You have available to them. May the eyes of their understanding be enlightened (Eph 1:17); that they may know how to gaze (PS 27:4) upon You in spirit and truth. This I do pray, in the precious name of Jesus. Amen.

Chapter 2
DESIRE

You have given him his heart's desire,
and have not withheld the request of his lips.

Psalm 21:2

We have just learned in the last chapter, that we must know what He says in His *Word*. Without knowing His *Word*, we really don't know Him. It's prevalent that we live by trust and faith in the Word of God, NOT by what we *see*. Yet, as we know what the Word of God says, we can distinguish what's not seen and yet exists in Heaven, and it will become our hearts *desire* that we may actually see it. We find promises in the *Word* of God that if we delight ourselves in Him, He will give us the *desires* of our heart (Ps 37:4). Whatever He has said, is real, and we must be able to see it as real. Let's look at 2Corinthians 4:18 NIV:

> So we fix our eyes not on what is seen, but on what is unseen, since what is seen is temporary, but what is unseen is eternal.

We must be careful to *desire* spiritual gifts with the correct mindset. I have found that as I have desired spiritual gifts, which we're commanded to do (1Cor 14:1), that they come with some interesting qualities that I did not foresee. For example, when we *desire* to really know Him, we must be willing to have our lives, our thoughts, and our actions interrupted at any given moment. If we truly want to know Him, a relationship must be formed, and we must give Him free access into our lives. We will need to allow Him to speak to us on His time table. In other words, we have got to become *available* to Him 24/7. If you've read any of my other books, you would have read where I like to say, "While I was - *minding my own little business*," He suddenly and seemingly out of nowhere, overwhelms me with His Presence, and I must fall to my knees and begin to pray. He also causes me to notice someone while I am out in public, and gives me an encouragement for them, or even prompts me to pray for them right on the spot. I don't say these things to startle you, but rather prepare you. You can't have relationship if you don't allow the other person to speak into your life freely.

If we have built a relationship with the Holy Trinity, it will bring trust in His *Word*, and the *Word* will take us into His heavenly realm. Actually, with relationship we can enter in at any given moment because the Kingdom of God is within us (Lk 17:21), or He can quicken us and reveal what He needs us to do, say, see, or pray, if we delight ourselves in Him. Let's look at Psalms 145:19:

> He will fulfill the *desire* of those who fear Him; He also will hear their cry and save them.

As I was studying this verse, I was reminded that the word *fulfill* {H6213} carries with it the meaning of not only - *to do*, but also that God will *fashion* or *make it*. So, if we *desire* to *meet with Him*, He is going to make it happen! That's why He created man, to have someone to commune with and as in the Garden of Eden, to walk with in the cool of the day. Let's look at that verse in Genesis 3:8-10:

> And they heard the sound {*voice*} of the Lord God walking in the garden in the cool {*wind, breeze*} of the day, and Adam and his wife hid themselves from the presence of the Lord God among the trees of the garden.

We know this story, but have we ever stopped to think that God could do the same with us? They were in the Garden of Eden, which God had created or planted Himself (Gen 2:8). Everything that God made was very good (Gen 1:31). If the Garden of Eden was so wonderful, just think of what we have on the inside of us – the Kingdom of God (Lk 17:21)! Let's look at what Romans 14:17 has to say about the Kingdom of God, which is within us.

> …for <u>the kingdom of God</u> is not eating and drinking, but *righteousness* and *peace* and *joy* in the Holy Spirit.

This points us to where our righteousness, peace, and joy in the Holy Ghost comes from – the Kingdom of God – which is in you and me. Glory! We have free access with no appointed hours or time limits to our Heavenly Father, and we should *desire* to do the same for Him also. Our *desire* should be to cry out to Him, and have Him call out to us. He will hear us when we call (Ps 34:17), and before we even ask, He will answer (Isa 65:24).

Do you have the *desire* to come boldly to His throne? If our *desires* are on earthly things, we will never set aside private time to *meet with Him*. We will allow our duties, work, and worldly *desires* to take up the time that we could have set apart for Him to manifest Himself to us. Our availability to Him is a key to building the relationship which we should all *desire* and crave.

Oh, that we would be as King David and allow our *desire* to be towards Him continually. Or like Moses and say if His Presence doesn't go with or lead us, we will not go either (Ex 33:15). This Presence is not only His Presence within each of us, but a *knowing* that His Presence is leading us. See, if we *desire* His Presence more than anything or anyone else, He will come and make Himself known to us. This *desire* is nothing more than a true, sincere love for the Holy Trinity. Did not the *Word* state that if we love Him, we would obey His commandments? He commands us to seek ye first the Kingdom of God and His righteousness (Matt 6:33). Let's look at John 14:19-21 AMPC:

> Just a little while now, and the world will not *see* Me anymore, but *you will see* Me; because I live, you will live also.
>
> At that time [when that day comes] you will know [for yourselves] that I am in My Father, and you [are] in Me, and I [am] in you.
>
> The person who has My commands and keeps them is the one who [really] loves Me; and whoever [really] loves Me will be loved by My Father, and I [too] will love him and will show (reveal, manifest) Myself to him. [*I will let Myself be clearly seen by him and make Myself real to him.*]

Do we *desire* for Him to make Himself clearly seen by us, for Him to make Himself real to us? Maybe we should see what this word *desire* actually means. Here is the Webster's Revised Unabridged Dictionary definition of *desire*:

Webster's Revised Unabridged Dictionary:

1. To long for; to wish for earnestly; to covet.

2. To express a wish for; to entreat; to request.

3. To require; to demand; to claim.

4. To miss; to regret.

5. The natural longing that is excited by the enjoyment or the thought of any good, and impels to action or effort its continuance or possession; an eager wish to obtain or enjoy.

6. An expressed wish; a request; petition.

7. Anything which is desired; an object of longing.

8. Excessive or morbid longing; lust; appetite.

DESIRE, noun

1. An emotion or excitement of the *mind*, directed to the attainment or possession of an object from which pleasure, sensual, intellectual or spiritual, is expected; a <u>passion excited by</u> the <u>love</u> of an object, or

uneasiness at the *want* of it, and directed to
its attainment or possession. ---

WOW! Do we actually have these feelings of *desire* for
Him? An emotion or excitement of the *mind* (where we
visualize Him), and *passion* excited by *love*; an earnest
longing! I must confess, that I truly long to be in His
Presence. In His Presence is fullness of joy (Ps 16:11).
There are no earthly words to describe what His
Presence is really like. I am praying that by the time
you're finished with this book, that you will truly know
and continually experience the joy of His Presence.

Here are a few verses that were linked to the previous
definitions:

Proverbs 19:2 AMPC:
Desire without knowledge is not good …

Job 20:20:
Because he knows *no quietness* in his heart, he will
not save anything he *desires*.

Song of Songs 7:10:
I belong to my beloved, and his *desire* is for me.

Proverbs 10:24:
The fear of the wicked will come upon him and
the *desire* of the righteous will be granted.

Psalms 40:8 NIV:

"I *desire* to do your will, my God; your law is within my heart."

Isaiah 26:8 AMPC:

Yes, in the path of Your judgments, O Lord, we wait [expectantly] for You; our heartfelt *desire* is for Your name and for the remembrance of You.

Prayerfully we can now see just how important our *desire* is towards Him. We have read where He wants to make Himself real to us, to manifest Himself to us (John 14:21). That word *manifest* {G1718} carries with it the meaning:

1. to manifest, exhibit to view

2. to show one's self, come to view, appear, be manifest

3. to indicate, disclose, declare, make known

God's *Word* says what it means, and means what it says. We can actually use our God given imagination to see Him for Who He is. If our *desire* is towards Him, and we know His *Word*, then He will show Himself to us. He will make Himself real to us, through our mind's screen. We simply need *desire*.

We read in His *Word* where it tells us that His eyes are like fire (Rev 2:18). We can actually see His eyes of fire as we read that verse. That's our God given imagination.

Another verse also states that His eyes are like fire, and His hair is white like wool (Rev 1:14). We can see that verse come to life with our imagination also. One particular verse I really like is speaking of when His glory (Presence) filled the temple and looked like a cloud (2Chro 5:14). As we imagine these verses coming to life as we read them, so can we *desire* that He invades our thought life to make Himself known to us through our imagination. We may or may not see Him manifested in these very ways, but if we don't know the *Word* of God, we will possibly miss how He is trying to reveal Himself to us.

We read in 1John 2:17 (CJB) "And the world is passing away, along with its *desires*. But whoever does God's will remains forever." What a promise! Whatever we *desire* that's worldly will pass away, but whatever we *desire* that's Godly will remain forever! As we build a relationship with the Holy Trinity, we are storing up treasures in Heaven. We will actually stand before Jesus and hear Him say, "Enter in, thou good and faithful servant." All because we have taken the time to get to know Him as He is.

As we have welcomed Him in to have 24/7 access to us, we're growing in love for Him day by day, even moment by moment. As previously stated, love is the key. If we truly love someone, then we are all about what they *desire*, what their needs are. We want to know every detail of how they think, how they react, what they like or dislike. Love brings with it that longing to be near and with that person. He has

His part paid in full. Are we going to accept His gracious gift of entering into a loving relationship with Him? A relationship without hesitations or exceptions.

Exceptions brings me back to knowing what we are asking for when we ask. As previously stated, I *desired* His gifts as He has commanded, but did not know what came with those gifts. We are not to limit Him on what part of a particular gift we *desire*. We receive the whole gift and not bits and pieces. We definitely should *desire* to see Him as He is, and at the same time, we cannot limit Him to how we see Him. If flaming eyes of fire startles you, He will not manifest Himself to you in that manner. He *desires* to meet with you, therefore He will meet you where you are spiritually.

He meets with us on the spiritual level we are on. We are not to be timid or fearful of the encounters we will have with Him. He reveals himself to us as we see Him through our imagination. However you see Him with your imagination, is the way He is presenting Himself to you. You are seeing Him clearly through how you have perceived Him from His *Word*. Now, He will not leave us at the level we are on. He will gently nudge us to bring us into a deeper relationship with Him. As we grow in knowledge of His *Word*, we grow in the wisdom of Who He is, and so our *desire* is for a new encounter with Him.

The steps in each chapter of *Meeting with God* are vital to growing a deeper relationship with Him. Stay with me through each chapter as we, together, walk out our pathway to *meet with God*. I sense you are wanting to jump to the last chapter! Please do not. I too am *desiring* to take you straight into *meeting with God*. However, the steps in these chapters are our source to a true and real encounter with the Holy Trinity. I know how it is to want to have it now. To *desire* an encounter with Him now, or receive a certain gift now, but experience or gifting without knowledge is not wise.

Once again we must know the *Word* of God to know who we are in Him. He then can reveal our heart's *desire* to us. He has placed this *desire* (Jer 24:7) in us, all for Himself. He wants our *desire* to grow for Him (Eph 1:17), even more than we do. Remember that no matter how much we are yearning and craving to be in His Presence, He *desires* it even more (2Chro 16:9). Therefore we can trust that as we are patient with the steps listed as chapters in this book, we will meet our hearts *desire* as we come face to face with Him.

Let's recap. The first chapter we learned the importance of knowing His *Word* in order to know Him, and how to build a deeper relationship with Him. In this chapter we have learned how our *desires* can be towards this world and will pass away, but as we place our focus on *desiring* what He wants us to *desire*, we will be storing up treasures in Heaven. He knows our thoughts from a far off (Ps 139:2).

As we come to the close of this chapter, may we understand that our *desires* will continue to increase as we increase in the knowledge and love of Him. Let's ask ourselves, "Are our *desires* towards Him continually?" Only we can answer that. The Holy Trinity knows our heart. They will draw us unto Themselves. Now maybe we can see that chapter one and two go hand in hand. No *Word*, no *desire*. The *Word* causes us to *desire* what we read and perceive of Him.

Let's pray:

> Father God, thank You for giving us our hearts *desire* (Ps 37:4). Help us to continue to earnestly *desire* Your gifts (1Cor 14:1). We want to be led with a deep *desire* to know You more. May our longing for Your Presence show You our true love for You. May Your *Word* come alive that we might *desire* to see You as You are. Thank You that our *desires* are Your *desires*. Father, we do truly *desire* to be in Your Presence, which brings us fullness of joy (Ps 16:11). This we do pray in the name of Jesus. Amen.

Chapter 3

PREPARE YOUR HEART

---

*LORD, You have heard the desire of the humble; You
will prepare their heart; You will cause Your ear to hear...*

Psalm 10:17

As we begin this chapter, let's start by searching the
meaning of the word *heart* in the above verse, from the
Strong's Concordance. I was pleasantly surprised to find
that it not only refers to the heart, but also to our mind.
As we go through this chapter we will learn just how our
mind comes into play when it's focusing on the Holy
Trinity. Here is its meanings:

Heart {H3820}:

1. inner man, *mind*, will, heart, understanding

   a. inner part, midst

      i. midst (of things)

      ii. heart (of man)

      iii. *soul*, heart (of man)

      iv. *mind*, knowledge, *thinking*, reflection, *memory*

      v. inclination, resolution, determination (of will)

      vi. conscience

      vii. heart (of moral character)

      viii. as seat of appetites

      ix. as seat of emotions and passions

         1. as seat of courage

When we say the word *heart* as a Christian, we are saying our inner man. And who is our inner man, but our spirit-man. Ephesians 3:16-17 explains more of what we are discussing, however let's read the verses surrounding it. The Apostle Paul is speaking in Eph 3:14-21:

For this reason I bow my knees to the Father of our Lord Jesus Christ, from whom the whole family in heaven and earth is named, that He would grant you, according to the riches of His glory, to be strengthened with might through His Spirit in the *inner man*, that Christ may dwell in your hearts through faith; that you, being rooted and grounded in love, may be able to comprehend with all the saints what *is* the width and length and depth and height— to know the love of Christ which passes knowledge; that you may be filled with all the fullness of God.

Now to Him who is able to do exceedingly abundantly above all that we ask or think, according to the power that works in us, to Him *be* glory in the church by Christ Jesus to all generations, forever and ever. Amen.

That is a lot of promise there in those verses. As a side note, that word *might* carries with it the meaning of *miraculous power*! We have power that we don't know or understand. Moving onto our focus, which is our heart or inner man. Ephesians 3:16-17 states, "that He would grant you, according to the riches of His glory, to be strengthened with might through His Spirit in the *inner man*, that Christ may dwell in your hearts through faith." It's through faith that we will connect with the Holy Trinity. We all know without faith it is impossible to please God. Let's take a look at that verse Hebrews 11:6 AMP:

> But without faith it is impossible to [*walk with God* and] please Him, for whoever comes [*near*] to God must [*necessarily*] believe that God exists and that He rewards those who [earnestly and diligently] *seek* Him.

Coming into the Presence of God surely requires faith. We have all been given the measure of faith (Rom 12:3), not to boast in ourselves, but to the glory of Him that gave it to us. Therefore, we can come boldly before Him, and especially in our time of need (Heb 4:16). We cannot boast in ourselves as if our own ability brought us unto Him, but that our needfulness of Him, in obedience to His *Word*, gives us free access, for which I am so grateful. Once we build relationship with Him, we know the price Jesus paid to be able to send us Holy Spirit, and how Father God was separated from His Son for us! All - that we could commune with Them, which when we think or meditate on that, should bring tears to our eyes.

To get to this type of relationship we must be spiritually minded and not naturally minded. We read that in the last chapter. Before we go any further, let's look at 1Corinthians 2:9-14:

> But as it is written: Eye has not seen, nor ear heard, nor have entered into the *heart* of man the things which God has prepared for those who *love* Him.

But God has *revealed* them to us through His Spirit. For the Spirit searches all things, yes, the deep things of God. For what man knows the things of a man except the spirit of the man <u>which is in him</u>? Even so no one knows the things of God <u>except the Spirit of God</u>. *Now we have received, not the spirit of the world, but the Spirit who is from God*, <u>that we might know</u> the things that have been freely given to us by God. These things we also speak, not in words which man's wisdom teaches but which the Holy Spirit teaches, comparing spiritual things with spiritual. But the natural man does not receive the things of the Spirit of God, for they are foolishness to him; nor can he know them, because they are spiritually discerned.

These verses clearly teach us that we do have the mind of Christ (1Cor 2:16), if His Spirit reveals unto our hearts, what His mind is. Again, knowing His *Word*, is vital, because He is going to speak to us and reveal Himself to us according to His *Word*. Romans 8:6 states. "For to be carnally minded is death, but to be spiritually minded is life and peace."

God is Spirit, and those who worship Him must worship in spirit and truth (John 4:24). We have got to train ourselves to become spiritually minded, because God lives in the spiritual realm. It sounds strange, but we have to build relationship with the invisible Spirit of God. John 14:20 states, "At that day you will know that I am in My Father, and you in Me, and I in you." This verse clearly tells us that Jesus is in the Father, and we are in Him, and He is in us! Our *heart* or inner spirit-man is connected with His Spirit.

To know this, we have to develop a clean conscience with our spirit-man. The word conscience means: internal or self-knowledge, or judgment of right and wrong; or the faculty, power or principle within us, which decides on the lawfulness or unlawfulness of our own actions and affections, and instantly approves or condemns them. To become God-conscience, we have to obey Philippians 2:12b AMPC:

> … work out (cultivate, carry out to the goal, and fully complete) your own salvation with reverence *and* awe and trembling (self-distrust, with serious caution, tenderness of conscience, watchfulness against temptation, timidly shrinking from whatever might offend God and discredit the name of Christ).

We should be working with the Christ in us to have Him manifest on our outward man, becoming strong in the spirit, as we serve the Lord. The weaker our spirit-man is the harder it is to receive the things of Him spiritually. When our spirit-man is weak, we're susceptible to oppression and depression. But if our inner man, our spirit-man is strong it is easier to fight off the wiles of the enemy. You and only you can keep your own spirit strong. It requires time and willingness to do the *Word* of God. We must feed our spirit-man daily. Even our outer man does not live by bread alone (Matt 4:4). Every day we must feed our spirit. Our spirit-man delights in the Law of God (Rom 7:22).

We are commanded to let the *Word* of God dwell richly in us in all wisdom (Col 3:16), reading and meditating on the *Word*. We simply read His *Word* and let Him quicken us to what He wants to reveal to us. That's building relationship. The more our spirit-man is exposed to Him and His quickenings, the stronger we get, simply waiting on Him to become real to us (Isa 40:31). As we wait, expecting to have an encounter with Him, He comes and we increase in our spirt-man. We read in 2Corinthians 3:18 where it states, "But we all, with unveiled face, beholding as in a mirror the glory of the Lord, are being transformed into the same image from glory to glory, just as by the Spirit of the Lord." It takes quality time to build relationship.

If we have built relationship with the Trinity, and we are in our congregational church service, we are then exposed to His Presence, and an encounter is up to us. There's a congregational anointing, and we can tap into it if we have built relationship with the Holy Trinity. In 1Corinthians 14:4 it states, "He who speaks in a tongue edifies himself, but he who prophesies edifies the church." That's simply praying in the Spirit. We connect with the Lord by praying in the Spirit, which builds up our most Holy faith (Jude 20). Praying in the Spirit produces power in our spirit-man. It also builds our faith, and it takes faith to connect with the Holy Trinity, just as it took faith to believe that He forgave our sins, and now abides in us.

We also strengthen our spirit-man by partaking of Holy Communion. We must partake with a clean conscience, remembering the blood shed, which was also for our ability to commune with Him. Jesus was our blood sacrifice that we may enter into the Holy of Holies freely. As we sow into spiritual promises, we reap spiritual blessings.

Quality time spent with the Holy Trinity is key to all the ways we strengthen our spirit-man. We must spend quality time alone with Him—in His *Word*—praying in the spirit, and also sowing into others. This causes our amour of light to increase. Walk in the light as He is in the light (1John 1:7). Be strong in the Lord and the power of His might (Eph 6:10). How much time do we actually give to these things? We must make these priority to survive in these last days!

We read in 1Corithians 2:9, "But as it is written: Eye has not seen, nor ear heard, nor have entered into the heart of man the things which God has prepared for those who love Him." We do have the mind of Christ (1Cor 2:16). He knows everything and He's all mighty and all powerful. He has revealed the riches of the glory of this mystery to us (Col 1:26-27). In Him is hidden all the treasures of wisdom and knowledge, we walk in Him, and we are complete in Him (Col 2:3, 6,10).

We must continue to *look unto* Jesus Who is the author and finisher of our faith (Heb 12:2). He can help us *not* to look at the things which are seen, but at the things which are not seen, because the things which are seen are temporary, but the things which are not seen are eternal (2Cor 4:18). This requires faith to *see* the unseen.

Jesus is always in us and we can imagine Him— *looking unto Jesus* (Heb 12:2). Jesus lives in us. He dwells there by faith (Eph 3:17). Let's not let the stumbling stone of unbelief stop us as it did the Israelites. Israel was pursuing the law of righteousness, but they could not attain it. Why? Because they did not seek it by *faith*. They sought it by the works of the law, therefore they stumbled at that stumbling stone of *faith* (Rom 9:31-32).

We have attained in the last chapter that our imagination was God-given. When our heart, mind and imagination is turned unto Jesus, the veil is taken away. How do we look to the Lord? How do we look unto Jesus the author and finisher of our faith? If I ask you to look up from reading, you can do that. But if I say look to the Lord, how do you do that? Though we may have questions, there are lots of scriptures that command us to *look unto Jesus*.

One easy way to explain how to look unto Jesus is to look at our minds as having a screen, like a movie, or projector screen. We ourselves can paint a picture there on the screen of our minds. Now, since Christ lives in us, He too can put anything He wants on the same screen. However, there is a third party that can throw images on our screen. That's the enemy and his demonic spirits, but we are no longer blinded by his evil ways.

We read in 2Corinthians 3:18 KJV, "We all, with open face beholding as in a *glass* the glory of the Lord, <u>are changed into the same image</u> from glory to glory, even as by the Spirit of the Lord." We are being transformed by His *Word* and unbelief is taken away because of faith in His promised *Word*. That word *glass* {G2734} means to show in a mirror or to make to reflect, and is derived from *kata* {G2596} which carries with it the meanings of varied relations, beyond measure, distribution, or intensity. It's also derived from the root word *optanomai optomai* {G3700} which carries with it the meanings of a middle voice, to look at, behold, to allow one's self to be seen, to appear, to gaze, continued inspection, as in voluntary observation.

We also see the word *glass* in 1Corinthians 13:12 KJV, "For now we see through a *glass*, darkly; but then face to face: now I know in part; but then shall I know even as also I am known." That word *glass* {G2072} is also mirror and also carries with it the {G3700} *optanomai optomai* meanings, and is from a root word *eis* pronounced as ice, and carries the meanings of into, unto, to, towards, for, among. All of which mean the point reached or entered, and *expressing motion* – thus the movie in our minds.

It takes faith to see Him. We have visionary capacity to see with our imagination. The word *see* {G3708} is *horáō* – properly, *see*, and is derived from the same word *glass* {G3700}. The word *see* carries a metaphorical meaning: "<u>to see with the mind</u>" (i.e. spiritually see), i.e. perceive (with <u>inward spiritual perception</u>). The meaning is to discern clearly (physically or mentally), to experience, passively to appear, behold, perceive, see, take heed.

We must consecrate (set apart) the eyes of our heart to the Lord. God gave us our imagination and we are to use it to communicate with Him. He created us that way so He can talk to us through our internal screen. He is going to show us things through our imagination. Where do we think God given ideas come from, and how do we perceive, or get them? He gives them to us through our imagination screen!

The *eyes* {G3788} of our heart is mentioned in Ephesians 1:18, and means the eye, and metaphorically *the eyes of the mind*, the faculty of knowing. We control what we put on our screen (*the eyes of our mind*). Whichever way we visualize Jesus is how we put Him on our screen, looking unto Jesus, simply with the eyes of your heart. We naturally do this as we read the *Word*. Like a verse where He is sitting in the boat on the shore. We have projected Him onto our screen in our mind.

Even as we, by faith, accepted Jesus as Lord of our life, we now, by faith, have to do something. We have to *look unto the Lord*. As we train ourselves to do this, it will become natural to us. When we look to the Lord, we connect with the Spirit and we get a projection from the other side! If we continue to behold the image of Jesus that we have now, then He will begin to change, and show us things. It's as simple as that! We look and turn our heart unto Jesus with our mind's screen.

Remember, we have got to discipline ourselves to look unto Him consistently. If we read Revelation 1:10-12, we read where John was in the Spirit on the Lord's Day. Look at the three steps John (*beholding Him*) encountered:

1) In the Spirit

2) Heard a voice

3) Looked and saw

We see this again in Revelation 4:2 – in the Spirit, saw, and heard in the Spirit. Faith is believing that it's not just your own imagination, but being God conscious by focusing on Him in love and worship. This connects our spirit-man to Him, and things begin to happen! First be in the Spirit—connect with Him, listen for instruction, and see where He wants to take you. John's next instruction was to write what he saw, and so should we.

It's important that we sanctify this area. We control what goes up on our screen. What we read, hear, and see can be brought up and projected on the screen. We have to be careful what we allow. What we focus on, we tune into. If we throw a sinful image up, then a demonic spirit is there to entertain that image. We must continually be casting down vain imaginations (2Cor 10:5). If the image is negative, remove it by refocusing Jesus back on the mind's screen.

Philippians 4:8 tells us to focus on whatever is pure, lovely, of good report. We know that God will never show us anything contrary to His *Word*. We've got to keep our screen clean, so God can speak to us and show us things. We read where John was told to write what he saw and heard. I strongly suggest we do the same. Keeping a journal of our encounters seems to tell Holy Spirit, that we honor Him talking to us, and showing us things.

As we work with Him it will become easier and easier. Quite often He will take us through a series of pictures as He trains us to follow his lead. He increases our visualization as we are diligent to spend quality time with Him. We must develop this, if we want a strong spirit-man.

As we come to a close of this chapter allow me to address past, bad images. The enemy will throw those up when there's a trigger for them. Sometimes it's like a movie that plays over and over. That's a problem, because he is using our screen and we can't seem to shut him off. To rid our self of this evil spirit's right to do this, we must take it to God and forgive anyone, and even our part in it. We must repent to obtain absolute cleansing. The power of God can wipe this out, erase the tape, and it can happen at the communion table. We simply focus on the body bruised, the blood shed, and see His sacrifice as cleansing our mind's screen. As we partake, we should use our mind's screen to see the life in the blood eradicating those past, bad images. We want a clean conscious and a clear heart. How do we *prepare our heart*? Simply looking unto Jesus!

Let's pray in agreement:

> Oh Father, as we enter into our secret place (Ps91:1) with You, we pray, our Father which art in Heaven, Holy is Your name, Thy Kingdom come, Thy will be done on earth as it is in Heaven (Matt 6:9-10). Enlighten the eyes of our heart (Eph 1:18) with spiritual eyes to see You clearly, and give us spiritual ears to hear what You are saying to us. Help us to cast down vain imaginations (2Cor 10:5), and to look unto Jesus Who is the author and finisher of our faith (Heb 12:2). We want to continually walk with a consciousness that You are in us, and that we have free access. Thank You Father, this we do pray in the name we look unto, Jesus. Amen.

Chapter 4
PREPARE A PLACE

But you, when you pray, go into your room,
and when you have shut your door, pray to your
Father who is in the secret place; and your Father
who sees in secret will reward you openly.

Matthew 6:6

As we read Psalms 91:1 we find that it states, "He who dwells in the *secret place* of the Most High Shall abide under the shadow of the Almighty." We have learned from the last chapter that we have free access to the Holy Trinity continually. We also learned how to enter into that *secret place*. So, my question to you is, "Do you have a *secret place* with Him?"

Our *secret place* should just be for Him. A *place* where we can go to *meet with Him*. A *place* where He knows that He has our undivided attention. A *place* without worldly distractions. The above verse states a room where we can close the door, and our Father will see us there, and even now, I can visualize Him smiling as His child is coming to *meet with Him*! He loves spending time with His children. He has things that He wants to convey to us, and through us. If He knows that we are going to be *meeting with Him*, He will be able to trust us with the secret things of His heart. He wants to be able to convey to us things in the earth that need prayer.

As we enter into our *secret place*, we're not to petition Him for ourselves, but to simply minister to Him and His needs. This *secret place* is in the natural, a physical *place* where we can get alone with God. Most men like to spend their time with Him while outdoors, or out of the house. It's harder for men to be still and know that He is God. Let's look at that verse. It's found in Psalms 46:10:

> Be still, and know that I am God; I will be exalted among the nations, I will be exalted in the earth!

> Psalms 46:10 ISV:
> Be in awe and know that I am God…

When we search out that word *still* {H7503} we find that it carries the meaning of: to relax, to be quiet. Even more exciting is that word *know* {H3045} which carries the meaning: to perceive, and *see*, find out, and discern! We definitely will not perceive, *see*, or find out anything with

God, if we do not quiet ourselves before Him. We read in Mark 6:31 where Jesus said to the disciples, "Come aside (apart) by yourselves to a deserted place and rest a while." We can get so busy doing Godly works, that we don't even have time to eat. It was true in Mark 6:31b which states, "For there were many coming and going, and they did not even have time to eat." What a trap of the enemy, but Jesus gave us the solution! Come apart!

The *Word* promises that there remains a rest for the people of God (Heb 4:9). In fact Hebrews 4:11 AMPC states, "Let us therefore be zealous and exert ourselves and strive diligently to enter that rest [of God, to know and experience it for ourselves], that no one may fall or perish by the same kind of unbelief and disobedience [into which those in the wilderness fell]. When we think of this word *rest* {G2663}, we think of the Sabbath rest, but this word also carries the meaning of: to pause. We must learn how to pause or rest before our Lord in our physical *secret place*. Time spent in our *secret place* will refresh us like nothing else!

Now in stating the importance of this rest before God, we cannot enter into it with fear. If we have a very hard time entering into rest, or being still, we may have some fear in our life. In 1John 4:18 we read:

> "There is no fear in love; but perfect love casteth out fear: because fear hath torment. He that feareth is not made perfect in love."

Fear hath torment, there's no rest or stillness if torment is present. Fear also translates to dread. If we are dreading something or someone, then we need to check our love walk. In other words, what does the *Word* of God say about the particular situation? No matter the situation, we always need to repent. Repent for allowing that tormenting spirit to enter in by fear and dread. We allowed it, and it will separate us from entering into the *secret place* spiritually. Don't allow condemnation to arise either, simply repent, and forgive them and/or yourself. Speak the *Word* of God over the situation, and allow the love of God to wash over you. There is no fear in God's love. Receive it and be free!

Now that we have fear taken captive (2Cor 10:5), let's discuss those random thoughts that try to invade our *secret place* time. As we are in our *secret place*, and we are focusing and worshipping Him from and with our heart/mind, most likely we will have random thoughts as we learn to enter in. These thoughts will not leave us alone until we write them down. Once we put them on paper, they cease to come to mind again. We may have several, and with each one, we must be sure to write them down quickly, so that those random thoughts do no steal our *secret place* time. The more we enter in, the easier it will become to just jot those thoughts down, and move on with God. Before long, we will be able to enter in with just a focus of His face, and nothing will distract us. It will be our choice to enter in or exit, simply by gazing upon His face.

There is a promise for those of us who wait on the Lord. Which is simply taking the time to enter into His Presence. We see that in Isiah 40:31:

> "But those who *wait* on the LORD shall renew their strength; they shall mount up with wings like eagles, they shall run and not be weary, they shall walk and not faint."

That's the rest of God! That word *wait* {H6960} carries the meaning: to wait, look for, hope, expect, and linger. Once again, with each word—to wait for, to look for, to hope, to expect, and to linger! I love those meanings. These are the things we need to be doing in our *secret place*. I can relate to each of these words. They seem to go in procession. Let's look at their order:

1. If we *wait* for Him,

2. We will *see* Him, and in *seeing* Him

3. We will have *hope* to *expect* Him to manifest Himself to us,

4. And in His Presence we will want to *linger*!

WOW! That's the God we serve. One Who speaks to us through His *Word* so that we may attain what is needed to enter into His Presence. His Presence is what we are after in our *secret place*. In His Presence He will speak to our hearts and write on our mind/screen the things He has for us at that time. In Matthew 5:8 we read:

> "Blessed are the pure in heart, for they shall see God."

This word *see* {G3708} is the same word we previously studied out in the last chapter with the actual meaning of: properly, *see*, often with metaphorical meaning: *to see with the mind*, (i.e. spiritually see), i.e. perceive (*with inward spiritual perception*). This verse is not only saying we will actually *see* Him in Heaven, in the hereafter, but that we may actually *see* Him now! But, there is a stipulation, it's only for those pure in heart. In the last chapter we also learned that we must obtain and keep a pure conscience if we are going to enter in. *Pure* {G2513} in heart carries the meaning of: clean, pure, unstained, either literally or ceremonially or spiritually; guiltless, innocent, and upright. To obtain this purity, we simply keep a clean slate before God with quick and sincere repentance.

In the Old Testament Chronicles we read where David prepared a *place* for the Ark of the Covenant. He prepared a *place* for God's Presence to rest or reside. As we *prepare a place* for Him, we must always be conscious that He lives on the inside of us (1John 4:13), and our *place of preparation* is for us to quiet ourselves and to learn to hear and see Him from within. This *secret place* is where He will teach us to enter into His Presence at any given moment ourselves, by simply looking unto Jesus (Heb 12:2), looking or gazing at His face. Now, when we can do this without even being still in our *secret place*, then He will begin to invade our minds as we go. Once again, if you know me or have read any of my books, you know I like to put Him invading my space like this, "*while I am minding my own little business*!" And He will do the same for you also.

Seemingly out of nowhere, He will invade our thoughts or place a picture on the screen of our mind, and we are to immediately begin to pray for the person or situation. Now, if we are not quick to be obedient, then He will pass that intercession onto someone who is. I so desire to be the one He counts on to intercede for others. When He brings intercession to me, it brings me a joy that I can't even describe. If you have not obtained this ability yet, be patient. Stay in your *secret place* as much as possible, and allow Him to teach you (1John 2:27). It comes by simply hearing, seeing, and being quick to be obedient.

S*eeing* or *hearing* was quite normal in the Bible. Peter, Paul, Joseph, and even Zacharias of the New Testament had visions, dreams, and visitations from angels. We too can prepare ourselves to receive from God, in any manner He chooses. It all starts by settling ourselves before Him consistently and obediently in our *secret place*. From there we can begin to have dreams of the night and visions during the day. Remember, we cannot make or cause these encounters to happen, we just position ourselves before Him, gaze upon Him, and allow Him to manifest Himself however He chooses. He wants to commune with us, and it's His job to train us in how He speaks to us individually. The hard part for us is to learn to be still and know (PS 46:10).

Again, it takes faith to enter into His Presence. Without faith we cannot please Him. But with faith, He is a rewarder to those who seek Him (Heb 11:6). As we consistently come before Him in faith, He will manifest Himself to us. Let's look at Hebrews 11:6 AMPC:

> But without faith it is impossible to please and be satisfactory to Him. For whoever would come near to God must [necessarily] believe that God exists and that He is the rewarder of those who earnestly and diligently seek Him [out].

I like what Hebrews 11:6 says in the ICB:

> Without faith no one can please God. Anyone who comes to God must believe that he is real and that he rewards those who truly want to find him.

God is real. Those of us who truly want to find Him have the promise that He will manifest Himself to us. Jesus promised that in John 14:21 which states:

> "He who has My commandments and keeps them, it is he who loves Me. And he who loves Me will be loved by My Father, and I will love him and *manifest* Myself to him."

That word *manifest* {G1718} carries the meaning: to show oneself, come to view, appear, and be manifest. As we wait patiently for the Lord, He will start a conversation with us. There's a verse found in Philippians 3:20 KJV which speaks of conversation:

> For our *conversation* is in heaven; from whence also we *look* for the Saviour, the Lord Jesus Christ:

That word *conversation* {G4175} translates citizen but comes from a root (G4176) and carries the meaning: *let conversation be, live*. I love that, our conversation is heavenly. Thy Kingdom come! The Kingdom lives within us (Lk 17:21). Glory! From our *secret place* that we have prepared just for Him and His Presence, we are learning to commune with the God of this universe! Then as we grow in the knowledge of how He speaks to us, we can take that *secret place*, which is truly *within* each of us wherever we go.

At the start of this chapter, I wanted to convey the importance of having a set-apart *place* to *meet with God*. It's in these meetings that we learn how He speaks to us individually. As we learn the ways He speaks to us, we then learn that the *secret place* is also within us. Even though we take the *secret place* that's within wherever we go, we can NOT omit the physical *secret place* meetings. If we do, we will slowly loose connection with Him. He is a jealous God, and wants our undivided attention. He is a loving Father, and fathers want to spend time with their kids. If we have genuinely come into His Presence through the *secret place*, then we are now ruined. From now on we will crave, desire, and long to be in His

Presence every moment that we can. And the good news is that at this point, we actually can be in His Presence with that overwhelming sensation He emits, just by focusing our attention – our mind's screen on Him! Looking unto Jesus!

Let's pray:

> Father God, thank You for meeting with us and for living on the inside of us (John 14:20). We are ever grateful to have free access to You (Eph 2:18). We want to continually dwell in the *secret place* (Ps 91:1). Your Word promises us dreams and visions (Acts 2/Joel 2), and may they begin out of our set-apart, *secret place* just for You. Train us to gaze upon Jesus, Who is the author and finisher of our faith (Heb 12:2). May we come boldly before You (Heb 4:16) with all confidence. This we pray in the name of Jesus. Amen.

Chapter 5
BONDSERVANT

---

*And if it happens that he says to you, 'I will
not go away from you,' because he loves you and
your house, since he prospers with you, then you shall
take an awl and thrust it through his ear to the
door, and he shall be your servant forever.*

Deuteronomy 15:16-17

The above verse is an Old Testament verse explaining
*bondservant*s. In the New Testament we are to become
bondservants to Jesus. We are to awaken each morning
seeking how to please our Lord. Deuteronomy 15:15
states, "You shall remember that you were a slave in the
land of Egypt, and the Lord your God redeemed you."
Egypt represents sin to us, therefore we are to remember
that He redeemed us from our sin, and in return we

should show our gratitude in serving Him wholeheartedly all the days of our lives (Duet 15:17). Verse 16 states, "And if it happens that he (*the bondservant*) says to you, 'I will not go away from you,' because he loves you and your house, since he prospers with you." Oh glory! The end of that verse states that the *bondservant* even prospers with the master, and so do we prosper with our Master.

We can't go any further till we see the meaning of a *bondservant* according to the Webster's 1828 Dictionary:

> BONDSERVANT, *noun* [bond and servant.] A slave; one who is subjected to the authority of another, or whose person and liberty are restrained.

This definition states that a *bondservant* is a slave who is subject to the authority of another person! Who wants to be a slave? No one, unless you are deeply in love with Jesus. The person who wants to follow Jesus wholeheartedly is the servant/slave of Him. He looks on our obedience (1Sam 15:22). As we serve Him with all that's within us, then He sees our wholeheartedness, and knows that He can trust us with anything. That's how we prove our servanthood to Him, and actually become His friend! That's building relationship with Him that He so desires of us.

If you are like me when I first read about being a *bondservant* or slave, I didn't like that title at all. However, the more I read and studied the Bible, the more in love I became with Jesus, and actually wanted to please Him in every area. I became a slave to Him, whom I grew to love with a deep and everlasting love. Let's look at some New Testament *bondservant* verses:

Romans 1:1:
Paul, a *bondservant* of Jesus Christ, called to be an apostle, separated to the gospel of God...

2Corinthians 4:5:
For we do not preach ourselves, but Christ Jesus the Lord, and ourselves your *bondservants* for Jesus' sake.

Galatians 1:10:
For do I now persuade men, or God? Or do I seek to please men? For if I still pleased men, I would not be a *bondservant* of Christ.

Ephesians 6:6:
... not with eye service, as men-pleasers, but as *bondservants* of Christ, doing the will of God from the heart...

Philippians 1:1:
Paul and Timothy, *bondservants* of Jesus Christ, to all the saints in Christ Jesus who are in Philippi, with the bishops and deacons...

Philippians 2:7:

…but made Himself of no reputation, taking the form of a *bondservant,* and coming in the likeness of men.

1Peter 2:16:

…as free, yet not using liberty as a cloak for vice, but as *bondservants* of God.

Now, from this standpoint we can see the obedience side of a *bondservant.* However, I want you to see where a *bondservant's* release was *totally up to him.* The verses below will also explain how a *bondservant* can truly fall in love with his master, who in turn becomes his saviour. Hopefully you are relating that with us and Jesus. These verses are so informative, and helpful in showing us that love through obedience is involved in being a true *bondservant,* all of which Jesus is looking for in us. We read about this in Deuteronomy 15:12-17:

If your brother, a Hebrew man, or a Hebrew woman, is sold to you and serves you six years, then in the seventh year you shall *let him go free* from you. And when you send him away free from you, you shall *not let him go away empty-handed*; you shall *supply* him liberally from your flock, from your threshing floor, and from your winepress. *From what the LORD has blessed you with, you shall give to him. You shall remember that you were a slave in the land of Egypt, and the LORD your God redeemed you;*

therefore I command you this thing today. And if it happens that he says to you, *'I will not go away from you,' because he loves you* and your house, since he *prospers with you*, then you shall *take an awl and thrust it through his ear to the door, and he shall be your servant forever.* Also to your female servant you shall do likewise.

I find it so interesting that the ear of the *bondservant* was thrust through on a door. See, Jesus is the door (John 10:9), and the ear represents us having the ability to *hear* from *Him*. This should be great news to us. In becoming a *bondservant* we show that we love and trust Him. We have drawn close to Him, how much more will He draw close to us? He can now trust us because we have proven ourselves as loyal servants. If we have made it to the point where we can say that we are His *bondservants*, then we can trust that He will lead us into an even deeper relationship with Him.

Many notable men of the Old Testament were referred to as servants. God spoke of Abraham as His servant (Gen 26:24). Moses also was called His servant (Num 12:7). Joshua is called the servant of the Lord (Joshua 24:29), as are David (2Sam 7:5), and Isaiah (Isa 20:3). Notable men in the New Testament used the word *bondservant*, slave, or servant and applied it to someone absolutely devoted to Jesus. Paul (Rom 1:1), Timothy (Phil1:1), James (James 1:1), Peter (2 Pet 1:1), and Jude (Jude 1:1). All describe themselves as "*bondservants* of Christ." Even Jesus Himself is called God's Servant (Isa 53:11). In all of these instances, the term servant carries the idea of humble nobility. Being God's servant is an honorable position, and Jesus represented His humble servanthood to His disciples and us, in John 13:3-5 AMPC:

> Jesus, knowing (fully aware) that the Father had put everything into His hands, and that He had come from God and was [now] returning to God,
>
> Got up from supper, took off His garments, and taking a [*servant's*] towel, He fastened it around His waist.
>
> Then He poured water into the washbasin and began to wash the disciples' feet and to wipe them with the [*servant's*] towel with which He was girded.

WOW! That should bring tears to our eyes, as we see where our Redeemer had taken on the role of a Servant. If we say we are in Christ, then we should consider ourselves *bondservant*s or slaves of Christ. He is our Lord, and our allegiance is due to Him alone. As *bondservants*, we renounce other masters (Matt 6:24) and give ourselves totally to Him (Matt 16:24). Let's take a look at some verses that tell us we should become a *bondservant* of Christ.

> 1Cor 7:22:
> For he who is called in the Lord while a *slave* is the Lord's freedman. Likewise he who is called while free is Christ's slave.

Eph 6:6:

…not with eye service, as men-pleasers, but as *bondservant*s of Christ, doing the will of God from the heart…

Being a *bondservant* of Christ is not drudgery. His "burden is light" (Matt 11:30). Also, we have this promise, "Now that you have been set free from sin and have become slaves to God, the benefit you reap leads to holiness, and the result is eternal life" (Rom 6:22). Hebrews 12:14 states, "Pursue *peace* with all people, and *holiness*, without which no one will see the Lord." Let's take a look at Hebrews 12:14-17 in The Message version:

Work at getting along with each other and with God. Otherwise you'll never get so much as a glimpse of God. Make sure no one gets left out of God's generosity. Keep a sharp eye out for weeds of bitter discontent. A thistle or two gone to seed can ruin a whole garden in no time. Watch out for the Esau syndrome: trading away God's lifelong gift in order to satisfy a short-term appetite. You well know how Esau later regretted that impulsive act and wanted God's blessing—but by then it was too late, tears or no tears.

There it is, peace and holiness, our road map into *meeting with Him*. Isaiah 26:3 states: "He will keep us in perfect peace as our *mind* is stayed on Him." The way to pursue peace and holiness, is simply by keeping our mind's screen on Him. Also, as the above verse states, "Keep a sharp eye out for weeds of bitter discontent. A thistle or two gone to seed can ruin a whole garden in no time." How true is that? Those verses also spoke of not letting a moment of pleasure stop us from enjoying the benefits of a *bondservant*. Regrets will hinder our ability to access all that is promised to us. With regrets, we will have a sense of un-holiness. That's a lie from the enemy. If we repent and turn towards Jesus, He is there with loving arms opened wide to welcome us in. Even without regrets and such, we tend to think that it is impossible for us to walk in holiness, but it's not. Let's look at what Easton's Bible Dictionary has to say about holiness:

> Holiness in the highest sense belongs to God (Isa 6:3; Re 15:4) and to Christians as consecrated to God's service, and in so far as they are conformed in all things to the will of God (Ro 6:19,22; Eph 1:4; Tit 1:8; 1Pe 1:15). Personal holiness is a work of gradual development. It is carried on under many hindrances, hence the frequent admonitions to watchfulness, prayer, and perseverance (1Co 1:30; 2Co 7:1; Eph 4:23-24).

We have just read where personal holiness is a gradual development. That's great news for us. Even though we may fail in an area, we still have the promise that Jesus became our righteousness (*right standing with God*), sanctification (*set apart for special use or purpose*), and redemption (*the work of Jesus on our behalf*). Let's look at some verses that will encourage us in the area of holiness:

1Cor 1:30:
But of Him you are in Christ Jesus, who became for us wisdom from God—and righteousness and sanctification and redemption—

John 17:19:
And for their sakes I sanctify Myself, that they also may be sanctified by the truth.

2Cor 7:1:
Therefore, having these promises, beloved, let us cleanse ourselves from all filthiness of the flesh and spirit, perfecting holiness in the fear of God.

Eph 4:23-24:
…and be renewed in the spirit of your mind, and that you put on the new man which was created according to God, in true righteousness and holiness.

Php 3:9:
and be found in Him, not having my own righteousness, which is from the law, but that which is through faith in Christ, the righteousness which is from God by faith;

From these verses we can know that we are in right standing with Jesus, and our deep love for Him makes us His *bondservant* if we commit our whole heart unto Him. In Matthew 11:29-30 Jesus states, "Take My yoke upon you and learn from Me, for I am gentle and lowly in heart, and you will find rest for your souls. For My yoke is easy and My burden is light." A yoke is a harness that straps around the shoulders of two animals to pull a plow or other heavy objects together. The two animals work in unison with one another. The word yoke of the Bible is a term that's used to describe submission. So when someone was described as being yoked to someone or something, it communicated the idea that he or she was submitting to that person or thing. So, to be yoked to Jesus is to serve and follow Him in total submission.

To be a *bondservant* to Jesus, means we lay down our will for His. He need not harness us to cause us to come in line with His *desires* for us, but rather we eagerly come to Him and place ourselves as His joyful servant. A *bondservant* who loves Him and His Kingdom is one who recognizes that they prosper with Him, and will gladly become His servant forever (Deut 15:17). A love slave to Jesus, acknowledges that they have nothing, and willingly gives everything back to Him. All that we have is His, and we are here for His good pleasure (Phil 2:13).

Just as the Old Testament *bondservant* had his ear lobe thrust through on the door post, we as New Testament *bondservant*s show our loyalty and love with our obedience to Him. If we are love slaves to Him, we will always have free access to Him. There will be no good thing that He'd withhold from us (PS 84:11). As we learned in a previous chapter, we can imagine and visualize Him anytime we want, and He can project anything He desires onto our mind's screen. As *bondservants*, our desire is to please our Master. Our hearts desire is in Him alone. Every choice we make is to please Him. He has left us His basic instructions in the *Word* of God of how to ultimately *meet with Him.*

Bondservant and obedience go hand in hand. In obedience we walk out our love for Jesus. As we are quick to be obedient to Him, I believe it opens us up to see Him clearer and clearer on our mind's screen. Since we have freely given ourselves back to Him, He then has a servant with a heart to please Him. If we look at a bond in the natural, it is where someone puts up money to set you free, and the money is like having insurance that you are not a flight risk. If we apply this to our relationship with Jesus, He did pay the price to set us free, and with the assurance that we will always be with Him! Just knowing He paid it all for us to be free in Him, is enough to cause us to be quick to be obedient to Him.

As we come to the close of this chapter, my prayer is that we now have a better understanding of what it means to be a true *bondservant* of Jesus. Without this type of love for Him, it would be doubtful that we'd feel worthy of the free access to Him, even though He paid the price in full. Simply surrender all to Him, and enter into all He has planned before the foundations of the earth. Let's look at that verse in Ephesians 1:4:

> Just as He chose us in Him before the foundation of the world, that we should be *holy* and without blame *before Him in love*...

Let's pray in agreement:

> Father God, we do thank You for choosing us before the foundations of the world, that we may be holy and blameless before Jesus in love (Eph 1:4). We surrender our lives unto You as *bondservants* to You forever (Deut 15:17). Help us to walk in complete obedience to You and Your ways (1Sam 15:22). Our desire is to please You, our Master. In the name that made it possible for us to become a *bondservant*, Jesus, we do pray. Amen.

Chapter 6

AVAILABILITY

So I sought for a man among them who would make a wall, and stand in the gap before Me on behalf of the land, that I should not destroy it; but I found no one.

Ezekiel 22:30

We most often read the above verse and instantly think of standing in the gap in prayer. Being a wall for someone, or filling in a breached hedge for someone or something is standing in the gap. However, today I want you to think of this verse in the light of the title of this chapter, *Availability*. When we research the word *stand* {H5975}, we find that the BDB Lexicon lists some interesting descriptive words: to tarry, remain, abide, endure, persist, and be steadfast. If we are wanting to ultimately *meet with God*, then we will need to be able to do each of these meanings behind the word *stand*.

Let's take the word *tarry* and find out what it actually means from the 1828 Webster's Dictionary and Thayer Lexicon:

TAR'RY, *verb intransitive*

1. To stay; to abide; to continue; to lodge.

   Tarry all night and wash your feet. Genesis 19:2.
2. To stay behind. Exodus 12:39.

3. To stay in expectation; to wait.

   Tarry ye here for us, till we come again to you. Exodus 24:14.

4. To delay; to put off going or coming; to defer.

   Come down to me, tarry not. Genesis 45:9.
5. To remain; to stay.

   He that telleth lies, shall not tarry in my sight. Psalms 101:7.

TAR'RY, *verb transitive* To wait for.

Thayer Lexicon: Luke 24:49

1. To make to sit down

   a. To set, appoint, to confer a kingdom on one

2. Intransitively

   a. To sit down

   b. To sit

      i. To have fixed one's abode

      ii. To sojourn, to settle, settle down

      iii. Luke 24:49: Behold, I send the Promise of My Father upon you; but tarry in the city of Jerusalem until you are endued with power from on high.

I suppose if we went through the rest of the word meanings for *stand* which are: remain, abide, endure, persist, and be steadfast, we'd find the same meanings as tarry. See, to be *available* to Him, it's going to take these actions. I guess my favorite definition would be *lodge*. If He lives on the inside of us, and He does (Gal 3:20), then He lodges in us, and we have free access to Him (Eph 2:18) at all times. To be *available* to Him, we must be able to focus all our attention on Him. We have previously learned that we can project Him on the screen of our mind. I do hope that you have been practicing this action. The more we can envision Him, the quicker we will be able to access Him, and the more He will be able to trust us to be *available* to Him.

You're probably wondering, "What's my being able to envision Him, got to do with Him seeing me as *available*?" I'm glad you asked! See, if we can see Him anytime we close our eyes, then the more we do this, the more things He is able to show us. Yes, He can see us as *available* by Him being allowed to lead us by His unction, but anyone who has the Spirit of God inside them has this ability. We call it intuition. However, for us to be *available* for Him to invite us into His realm, we must be visionaries. As we learn to tarry with Him, He has free access to our mind's screen and can project anything He needs us to see. When this type of relationship is established, He can then project a picture of the face of a person that needs prayer or a call of encouragement. This will happen as we go. You may be driving or doing your everyday chores. That's when you know that you have become *available* to Him. Like I like to say, *"As we are minding our own little business,"* He then invades our space, and our thoughts. Let's look at the definition of *availability*:

> Availability: noun
> * the quality of being <u>able to be used</u> or obtained.
>
> * the state of being otherwise <u>unoccupied</u>; <u>freedom to do something</u>.

The first definition is being able to be used or obtained. That's what we are aiming for. We want Him to be able to use us for His glory, and to do that, He must be able to obtain us when He needs us to do the work of the ministry here and now. The next definition seems a little harder, because we must be unoccupied by our everyday circumstances to be able to be *available* or free to do for Him when He calls. Neither of these definitions are going to come by a halfhearted commitment to building a sound relationship with the Trinity. That's why each of these chapters have been building up to this one.

Let me tell you how I came to be *available* to Him. I was at church at the altar worshiping, when our pastor heard the Lord speak, "Ask what you will and it will be given unto you." At that same moment I had turned to go back to my seat, when suddenly I was intoxicated with His Presence. I fell under the Power of God with my left arm in the air, and not wanting to move from His Presence. All the while, I'm trying to think of the right thing to ask God for, as He had just said to ask and it would be given. I tried to ask for my husband, for my son, for our ministry, and on and on. Each time I would mention one of these, God would say, "No, what do you want?" So out of desperation, I said to God, "I want what You want me to want." Immediately I heard, "*Availability.*" I cried and cried. Needless to say the whole service I was at the altar on my back with my left arm in the air. When I realized my arm was still in the air, I then saw with my mind's screen, an angel kneeling by me holding my arm up! People in the congregation that day saw the whole experience. That day, with such a God encounter, I was forever changed. I then started spending more time in prayer and listening for His voice in obedience to "*availability.*" Through that encounter, I have become more in tune with the ways of God. If you have read any of my previous books, then you know that I have always had an ear to hear Him, not of my own doing, and after this encounter with Him, it was to do as He leads me at any given moment – *availability*. Available to hear His leadings, and to speak what He is saying to His children, at all times.

In this chapter, we want to see the importance of being *available* to Him in light of the ultimate *meeting with Him*. Let's recap the previous chapters that have been leading up to this one. Each chapter is like a stepping stone to the next. The *Word* is our first chapter, and our very starting place. Without the *Word*, we will never get very far in life, or the ways of God. By His *Word* we learn who He is and how He speaks to us. The *Word* is our foundation that we continue to feed on. Next is *desire*, which we must have if we are ever going to *meet with Him*. As our *desire* to be with Him grows, we then must *prepare our heart* by His *Word* and in accordance to His *Word*. With these stepping stones in place, we then can move onto *preparing a place* to *meet with Him*. A *place* that is set apart for just Him. A *place* that when we go there, He then knows that we are coming to *meet with Him*. As we meet Him in this *place*, our love for Him grows to the point where we become a *bondservant* to Him. We have fallen so deeply in love with Him that we never want to be without Him being right here with us, which in turn causes us to always want to be *available* to Him.

As I was praying over this chapter, and asking Holy Spirit what He wanted to convey to His children, I kept saying the word, *inshallah*. In prayer, I sometimes get stuck on a word and seem to keep saying it. That's when

I know that He is trying to tell me something, so I write the word down and look it up afterwards. I then can return to praying. Well, when I looked up the word *inshallah* in Hebrew, I was pleasantly surprised, and you will be also. It was borrowed from an Arabic word and means: *With God's help*! WOW!

If you were wondering if you could ever be *available* to Him at all times, He is plainly telling you, "Yes." With His help, you will continue to grow in the steps of this book, and continue to please Him by *meeting with Him*, because you are *available* to Him. *Availability* calls for a lifestyle change. However, we cannot just jump into it without the other previous steps. With His help, we are growing in relationship and love for Him, which is leading us in His pathway for us to *meet with Him*. We not only already have intuition, but we have Him on the inside of us leading us to do, say, and go where He leads. We have trained our mind's screen to see Him anytime we close our eyes. Why do I say, "Close our eyes?" It's because when we close our eyes, we shut out the world around us, and we are able to focus on Him (Heb 12:2). As we get to the point where seeing Him with our imagination brings His Presence at that very moment, it's then that He knows we are truly *available* to Him. If we can close our eyes and are instantly overwhelmed by His Presence, then we can know that we have reached the ability to be *available* to Him.

Let's read where Peter was on the roof. In these verses, we can see where what we see with our mind's screen could be shrugged off as something natural, when it's actually Him conveying a thought to us. Let's look at Acts 10:9-16:

> [9] The next day, as they went on their journey and drew near the city, Peter went up on the housetop to pray, about the sixth hour.

> [10] Then he became very hungry and wanted to eat; but while they made ready, he fell into a trance

> [11] and saw heaven opened and an object like a great sheet bound at the four corners, descending to him and let down to the earth.

> [12] In it were all kinds of four-footed animals of the earth, wild beasts, creeping things, and birds of the air.

> [13] And a voice came to him, "Rise, Peter; kill and eat."

> [14] But Peter said, "Not so, Lord! For I have never eaten anything common or unclean."

> [15] And a voice spoke to him again the second time, "What God has cleansed you must not call common."

¹⁶ This was done three times. And the object was taken up into heaven again.

As we read this, we read where Peter was in prayer and initially very, hungry. God then shows him a sheet with animals/food on it. Peter did not shrug this off as him being naturally hungry, no! He had such a relationship built with the Holy Trinity that He *knew*, though at first it was animals he could not have, He had seen the will of God. This is exactly what this chapter is trying to convey. We must become so sensitively aware of His Presence, that we can be instantly invaded by Him, thus being *available*! And like Peter, naturally hungry or not, *available* at any given moment.

Let's look at Proverbs 20:12 and Psalms 94:9:

> Pro 20:12:
> The hearing ear and the seeing eye, The LORD has made them both.

> Ps 94:9:
> He who planted the *ear*, shall He not hear? He who formed the eye, shall He not see?

Both of these words for *eye* {H5869} and *ear* {H241} are the same in the Strong's for each verse. Let's look at what they represent:

BDB Lexicon: Eye H5869

1. eye

    a. eye

        i. of physical eye

        ii. as showing mental qualities

        iii. of mental and spiritual faculties (figuratively)

2. spring, fountain

BDB Lexicon: Ear H241

1. ear, as part of the body

2. ear, as organ of hearing

3. (subjective) to uncover the ear to reveal; the receiver of divine revelation

We find that the eye is of *mental* and *spiritual* faculties, and the ear is the receiver of *divine revelation*. The Lord hath made them both, both for us to perceive what He is saying and showing us, especially with our mind's screen when we are *available* to Him. We have these two verses as promises that He really wants to connect with us. What a comfort for those of us who are seeking His face with our whole heart.

Before we close out this stepping stone chapter, let's take a look at some scriptures that point to availability:

1Sam 3:10:

Now the LORD came and stood and called as at other times, "Samuel! Samuel!" And Samuel answered, *"Speak, for Your servant hears."*

Isa 6:8:

Also I *heard the voice of the Lord*, saying: "Whom shall I send, and who will go for Us?" Then I said, "Here am I! Send me."

Mark 1:17-18:

Then Jesus said to them, "Follow Me, and I will make you become fishers of men." They *immediately* left their nets and followed Him.

John 14:26:

"But the Helper, the Holy Spirit, whom the Father will send in My name, He will teach you all things, and *bring to your remembrance* all things that I said to you."

Luke 10:27:

So he answered and said, "You shall *love* the LORD your God with all your *heart*, with all your *soul*, with all your *strength*, and with all your *mind*, and your neighbor as yourself."

Rom 12:1:

I beseech you therefore, brethren, by the mercies of God, that you *present your bodies a living sacrifice,* holy, acceptable to God, which is your reasonable service.

As we come to a close of this chapter, may we earnestly seek His face, which in turn shows Him that we truly want to be *available* to Him. May we be as Peter on the roof that whether we are hungry or not, we still can be *available* for Him to speak to us through our mind's screen, or be led by His still small voice. May we be so in tune with Him that we are able to drop what we are doing and immediately follow His leading. This is a pivotal point in our adventure to *meet with Him*. Let's keep listening and being open to hear His still small voice (1Kings 19:12), and ever looking unto Jesus the author and finisher of our faith (Heb 12:2).

Let's pray:

> Holy Father God, thank You for making a way for us to boldly come before Your throne of grace (Heb 4:16). Enlighten our eyes to see who we are in Christ Jesus (Eph 1:18). Help us to always be *available* to your Presence in our lives (Ps 16:11). Show us how You speak to each of us individually. Help us to focus on You as we close our eyes, that we may instantly be in Your Holy Presence. We choose to always be available to You, teach us how to linger with You. We do ask these things in the Name above all names, Jesus. Amen.

Chapter 7

KNOCKING

Behold, I stand at the door and knock. If anyone hears My voice and opens the door, I will come in to him and dine with him, and he with Me.

Revelation 3:20

Let's start off with a story told by Jesus. He tells the story of a man and some of his friends. One of the friend's *knocked* on another friend's door at midnight. The friend in the home did not want to get up and do for his friend *knocking* on the door because he and his family were in bed. However, because of his *knocking* friend's persistence, he was persuaded and answered the door. Let's look at these verses in Luke 11:5-7:

And He said to them, "Which of you shall have a friend, and go to him at midnight and say to him, 'Friend, lend me three loaves, for a friend of mine has come to me on his journey, and I have nothing to set before him,' and he will answer from within and say, 'Do not trouble me; the door is now shut, and my children are with me in bed; I cannot rise and give to you?'"

Jesus goes on to tell us that that because of the *knocking* friend, the other friend gets out of bed and helps him, again, because of the *knocking* friend's persistence, which we can read in verse 8. If we then continue to read in Luke 11:9 and 10, we find that Jesus then goes straight into teaching us about asking, seeking, and *knocking*. Let's look at these verses in Like11:8-10:

> 8 "I say to you, though he will not rise and give to him because he is his friend, yet because of his persistence he will rise and give him as many as he needs.

> 9 So I say to you, ask, and it will be given to you; seek, and you will find; *knock*, and it will be opened to you.

> 10 For everyone who asks receives, and he who seeks finds, and to him who *knocks* it will be opened."

From this we have learned that by being persistent in asking, seeking, and *knocking*, we will be heard by Him. This is glorious news. However, how many of us can actually stay the course, by pressing in? If we were the *knocker* in this story, would we have *knocked* on our neighbor's door and took his word that he would not get up for us? If so, our want, our need, and our faith would be small. We actually need to pursue Jesus by loving Him with all our heart, soul, mind, and strength (Mk 12:30). There's a verse that's coming to my mind in Matthew 11:12 that states that the violent take the Kingdom of Heaven by force. In other words, we're not playing, or just trying, we are all out committed to *meeting with Him,* no matter the cost.

The next words Jesus uses is an illustration of an earthly father versus our Heavenly Father. We've all read these verses, but do we actually believe them? Either way, He is assuring us that our Heavenly Father is a good father (Ps 100:5; 33:5). Not only is God good, but He is love (1John 4:16). Let's read the verses from Luke 11:11-13 on an earthly father versus our Heavenly Father:

> [11] "If a son asks for bread from any father among you, will he give him a stone? Or if he asks for a fish, will he give him a serpent instead of a fish?
>
> [12] Or if he asks for an egg, will he offer him a scorpion?
>
> [13] If you then, being evil, know how to give good

gifts to your children, how much more will your heavenly Father give the Holy Spirit to those who ask Him!'"

See, we've got to be a persistent *knock*er through our prayer and *secret place* time with Him, and He being good and loving, will hear us and answer us (John 13:12-14). He promises to do this if we love Him and obey His commandants. As we learn to *knock*, we will then learn how to sense His *knocking* towards us. Let's look at yet another story told by Jesus that represents a persistent person. We find it in Luke 18:1-8:

> [1] Then He spoke a parable to them, that men always ought to pray and not lose heart,
>
> [2] saying: "There was in a certain city a judge who did not fear God nor regard man.
>
> [3] Now there was a widow in that city; and she came to him, saying, 'Get justice for me from my adversary.'
>
> [4] And he would not for a while; but afterward he said within himself, 'Though I do not fear God nor regard man,
>
> [5] yet because this widow troubles me I will avenge her, lest by her continual coming she weary me.'"

⁶ Then the Lord said, "Hear what the unjust judge said.

⁷ And shall God not avenge His own elect who cry out day and night to Him, though He bears long with them?

⁸ I tell you that He will avenge them <u>speedily</u>. Nevertheless, when the Son of Man comes, will He really find <u>faith</u> on the earth?"

If you recall in the previous story of the friends, I commented that if we had listened to the friend and left as he told us, "no," the first time then our need, want, and faith was small. The last verse above captures that remark. Remember we are to look to Jesus who is the author and finisher of our faith (Heb 12:2). If we were bold enough to go to a friend's home at midnight, then our want, need, and faith must be high.

Now in the story above with the widow and the unjust judge, we surely can see where perseverance is an asset. Jesus starts the parable off with, "That men always ought to pray and not lose heart (Lk 18:1)." Reminds me of the verse that states, "Let us not be weary in well doing: for in due season we shall reap, if we faint not" (Gal 6:9). God is looking for complete *availability* in us. He is expecting and even anticipating us to *knock*, so He can in turn *knock* back! Let's take a moment and read some asking verses to build our faith:

Matthew 7:7 AMPC:
Keep on asking and it will be given you; keep on seeking and you will find; keep on *knocking* [reverently] and [the door] will be opened to you.

Matthew 21:22 AMPC:
And whatever you ask for in prayer, having faith and [really] believing, you will receive.

Mark 11:24 AMPC:
For this reason I am telling you, whatever you ask for in prayer, believe (trust and be confident) that it is granted to you, and you will [get it].

John 15:7 AMPC:
If you live in Me [abide vitally united to Me] and My words remain in you and continue to live in your hearts, ask whatever you will, and it shall be done for you.

James 1:6 AMPC:
Only it must be in faith that he asks with no wavering (no hesitating, no doubting). For the one who wavers (hesitates, doubts) is like the billowing surge out at sea that is blown hither and thither and tossed by the wind.

1John 3:22 AMPC:
And we receive from Him whatever we ask, because we [watchfully] obey His orders [observe

His suggestions and injunctions, follow His plan for us] and [habitually] practice what is pleasing to Him.

Isaiah 55:6 AMPC:
Seek, inquire for, and require the Lord while He may be found [claiming Him by necessity and by right]; call upon Him while He is near.

1John 5:14-15 CJB:
[14] This is the confidence we have in His presence: if we ask anything that accords with His will, He hears us.
[15] And if we know that He hears us — whatever we ask — then we know that we have what we have asked from Him.

As far as parables and stories about persistence are concerned, we can go all the way back to Moses. He conveyed a message from God to Pharaoh. Moses prayed and spoke with God and as he did, God would give Moses the next step to convey to Pharaoh. From this story, we learn that if it's God's will, it will happen. This book is steps to *Meeting with God*. If we follow through, we will **know** that we have free access to Him at any time. Let's take a look at the verses about Moses and Pharaoh in Exodus 5:1:

Afterward (*a presentation to the leaders*) Moses and Aaron went in and told Pharaoh, "Thus says the

> Lord God of Israel: 'Let My people go, that they may hold a feast to Me in the wilderness.'"

From this we can see where God was *knocking* on Pharaoh's heart, but Pharaoh wasn't listening, and he paid the ultimate price. The verse that states, "It is better to obey than to sacrifice," (1Sam 15:22) is clearly seen in this story. God is always *knocking* on our hearts, yet we do not perceive Him. If that is the case then it's because we have not spent time in the *secret place* and in His *Word*, alone with Him. We must build a relationship that is a two way conversation. We do not want our conversation to be just us doing the speaking, but for Him to speak to us. That's what *meeting with God* is all about. We come before Him to minister to Him, to listen for His heart to be revealed to us (1Sam 3). The more He conveys His heart, the closer our relationship gets. We want to be *available* for Him to *knock* and to be quick to be obedient. Let's purpose in our heart to not only be a *knocker*, but to allow Him to *knock* on the door of our heart.

This chapter's heading verse was Jesus speaking in Revelation 3:20. In this verse, we read where we can commune with Him, if we answer His *knock*. Let's look at that verse and the cross reference verses to it. As we do, we will see a deeper revelation to this verse. We'll start with Revelation 3:20 AMPC, and then follow up with the reference verse.

Rev 3:20 AMPC:

Behold, I stand at the door and *knock*; if anyone hears *and* listens to *and* heeds My voice and opens the door, I will come in to him and will eat with him, and he [will eat] with Me.

Song 5:2:

THE SHULAMITE I sleep, but my heart is awake; it is the voice of my beloved! He *knocks*, saying, "Open for me, my sister, my love, My dove, my perfect one; for my head is covered with dew, My locks with the drops of the night."

Luke 12:37:

Blessed are those servants whom the master, when he comes, will find watching. Assuredly, I say to you that he will gird himself and have them sit down to eat, and will come and serve them.

John 14:23:

Jesus answered and said to him, "If anyone loves Me, he will keep My word; and My Father will love him, and We will come to him and make Our home with him."

Each of these verses are reminding us to be listening for His *knock*. We want our love for Him to overflow to others, but this will not happen if our relationship is not intimate. A shallow relationship is like an acquaintance we've met, where we do not really know them. Oh, maybe in name, but not intimately. Most Christians do the same with the Trinity. They know Them by name, but never spend time with Them. Thus, they never realize that the Holy Trinity is *knocking* on the door of their hearts daily.

In this chapter we have gone from us *knocking* on Heaven's door, to Heaven's Holy Trinity knocking on the door of our hearts. We know how to *knock* and reach out in prayer, but do we know how to sit quietly, ministering only to Him, and have Him come commune with us? That's our ultimate goal, to *meet with Him*. As previously stated, as we learn to be still before the Lord, we will gradually learn His *knock* on our heart. After we have perfected that, He will begin to *knock* on our heart, as we go. That's so awesome when we're, "*minding our own little business*," and He *knocks* on our heart with an impression, unction, urgency, or image on our mind's screen to reach out to someone, through the gifts of the spirit (1Cor 12:1-11). We may be prompted to pray immediately, to call or text someone with a word of encouragement, or lay hands on someone out in the public. However, we will not reach this point until we follow the steps which are listed in each chapter of this book. Let's recap those previous chapter titles, and ending with this one.

Chapter 1: *The Word*
Chapter 2: *Desire*
Chapter 3: *Prepare Your Heart*

As we have walked through each of these chapter titles, we are learning how to *enter into Heavenly places*, and ultimately *meet with God*. Each chapter builds upon the next. You may get to a chapter and think that you should just tarry there for a while, that's perfect. This means you know that you are hungry to grow in this area, and Holy Spirit will teach you as you ponder on that particular chapter (1John 2:27).

I have previously mentioned that we all want to bypass the steps, and go straight to *meeting with God*, however, we need the tools to enter in and have it be a lasting relationship built on love, obedience, and *availability*. Anything worth having is worthy of the cost. When we are willing to pay the price, we are stating that we hold something that is precious to us. It will cost us to be *available* to Him, however if we remember the scriptures, He has redeemed us by purchasing us with His very blood (Gal 3:13). He thought we were worthy of the cost! Therefore, whatever time we spend reading His *Word*, whatever time we spend fasting, whatever time we spend seeking Him, whatever time we spend listening for His still small voice, is worth the cost: plus, the rewards are precious.

As we come to the close of this chapter, may we all long to have Him *knock* on our hearts more than we *knock* on His door. The rewards of meeting with Him are many, for in His Presence is fullness of joy (Ps 16:11).

Let's pray:

> Heavenly Father, we truly thank You for Your Word made flesh that we may learn how to enter into Your Presence. Thank You for giving us eyes that see and ears that hear. Help us to long to have You *knock* on our heart, more than we *knock* on Yours. We want to hear and perceive what You are conveying to us. *Knock* on our hearts, Lord. This we do pray in the everlasting name above names, Jesus. Amen.

Chapter 8
ENTER INTO HEAVENLY PLACES

... while we do not look at the things which are seen, but at the things which are not seen. For the things which are seen are temporary, but the things which are not seen are eternal.

2 Corinthians 4:18

The title of this chapter, hopefully, piques your interest. To build our desire even more, let's see where we actually have access to the Holy Trinity. In the book of Ephesians *Heavenly places* is mentioned time and time again. Let's take the time to read each verse with our imagination. Let's put these verses on our mind's screen.

Eph 1:3:
Blessed be the God and Father of our Lord Jesus Christ, who has blessed us with every spiritual blessing in the *heavenly places* in Christ …

Eph 1:20:
which He worked in Christ when He raised Him from the dead and seated Him at His right hand in the *heavenly places…*

Eph 2:6:
and raised us up together, and made us sit together in the *heavenly places* in Christ Jesus…

Eph 3:10:
to the intent that now the manifold wisdom of God might be made known by the church to the principalities and powers in the *heavenly places…*

Eph 6:12:
For we do not wrestle against flesh and blood, but against principalities, against powers, against the rulers of the darkness of this age, against spiritual hosts of wickedness in the *heavenly places.*

So we need to ask the question where or what are *Heavenly places. Heavenly* in the Greek is G2032. Each time we read *heavenly places* above, they all had the same Greek word. Let's look at the {G2032} in the Strong's Lexicon.

1. existing in heaven

   a. things that take place in heaven

   b. the heavenly regions

      i. heaven itself, the abode of God and angels

      ii. the lower heavens, of the stars

      iii. the heavens, of the clouds

   c. the heavenly temple or sanctuary

2. of heavenly origin or nature

Heavenly places simply mean the realm of the spirit. It's important to understand that it's not just a *place* in *heaven* because we see that there are principalities and powers of evil forces also in *Heavenly places*. However, we know that there are no evil principalities and powers in heaven and there are no demonic forces in heaven, but in *Heavenly places*. Ephesians 3:10 specifically states: "to the intent that now the manifold wisdom of God might be made known by the church to the principalities and powers in the *heavenly places*." This verse is talking about the realm where powers and principalities reside, and shortly we will read where we are seated far above them. Praise the Lord!

Let's focus our understanding on the fact that *Heavenly places* is a spirit realm that is in us, and it's around us. When the scripture talks about *Heavenly places* it's talking about this realm in us and around us that extends from where we are and goes right through to *Heavenly places*. It's not a million miles away, but within us and around us.

From here we need to see how to take our Heavenly seat. A seat that is far above these powers and principalities. We have read where we are seated in *Heavenly places*. If you happen to be a WWP which stands for World Wide Prayer, then you pray this daily with Sister Billye Brim. Let's read how we can be seated in *Heavenly places*.

> Eph 1:17:
> that the God of our Lord Jesus Christ, the Father of glory, may give to you the spirit of wisdom and revelation in the knowledge of Him,
>
> [18] the eyes of your understanding being enlightened; that you may know what is the hope of His calling, what are the riches of the glory of His inheritance in the saints,
>
> [19] and what is the exceeding greatness of His power toward us who believe, according to the working of His mighty power
>
> [20] which He worked in Christ when He raised Him from the dead and seated Him at His right hand in the *heavenly places*,

²¹ far above all principality and power and might and dominion, and every name that is named, not only in this age but also in that which is to come.

²² And He put all things under His feet, and gave Him to be head over all things to the church,

²³ which is His body, the fullness of Him who fills all in all.

Eph 2:1:
And you He made alive, who were dead in trespasses and sins...

Eph 2:4:
But God, who is rich in mercy, because of His great love with which He loved us,

⁵ even when we were dead in trespasses, made us alive together with Christ (by grace you have been saved),

⁶ and raised us up together, and made us sit together in the *heavenly places* in Christ Jesus,

⁷ that in the ages to come He might show the exceeding riches of His grace in His kindness toward us in Christ Jesus.

⁸ For by grace you have been saved through faith, and that not of yourselves; it is the gift of God,

⁹ not of works, lest anyone should boast.

We see here that as long as Jesus is Lord of our life, then we are seated in the *Heavenly places* in Him. As we take our seat in the *Heavenly place* it's much like diving or swimming under the water. When we're under the water, we enter into another realm that sounds different, feels different, and looks different. However it's just another environment. *Heavenly places* in the kingdom of God is the realm of the spirit. It's like diving or swimming, we dive into another realm which is just as real as this realm, yet feels, looks, and sounds different.

Jesus said you can enter into the Kingdom of God now by being born again (John 3:5). However, being aware of it is another thing. We can read where Jesus was able to walk in this physical realm and the Heavenly realm spontaneously. In Ephesians 1:3 it states, "Blessed be the God and Father of our Lord Jesus Christ, who has blessed us with every spiritual blessing in the *heavenly places* in Christ." We read here that spiritual blessings are found in the realm of the spirit in *Heavenly places*. The favor of God is already laid aside for us; every spiritual blessing in the *heavenly places* in Christ. They are in the realm of spirit, where the favor of God and His blessing reside. I suppose we all have unclaimed blessings that God has purposed for us to have in this realm of the spirit called *Heavenly places*. I want all the blessing He has laid aside for me. How about you?

Now that we know these blessings are there according to the full knowledge of God, how do we release them? By seeing it in the spirit and by speaking it in faith, that's how we appropriate it. Our visionary capacity is our God given imagination. It bridges the gap between this physical realm and the spiritual realm. Whatever we focus upon in life is what we will connect with spiritually. When our focus is upon the Lord we connect with Him. To do this, we have to use our imagination, remember our mind's screen? Visualization is not a new age term it's a New Testament term. Let's read a few verses to help us with our God given New Testament imagination.

> 2Cor 3:18:
> But we all, with unveiled face, <u>beholding</u> as in a mirror the glory of the Lord, are being transformed into the <u>same image</u> from glory to glory, just as by the Spirit of the Lord.

> Isa 26:3:
> You will keep him in perfect peace, whose <u>mind</u> is stayed on You, because he trust in You.

> Heb 12:1-2:
> Therefore we also, since we are surrounded by so great a cloud of witnesses, let us lay aside every weight, and the sin which so easily ensnares *us,* and

let us run with endurance the race that is set before us, <u>looking unto Jesus</u>, the author and finisher of *our* faith, who for the joy that was set before Him endured the cross, despising the shame, and has sat down at the right hand of the throne of God.

In Philippians 3:20 KJV it states, "For our conversation is in heaven; from whence also we look for the Saviour, the Lord Jesus Christ." The Greek meaning of that word conversation, is the commonwealth of citizens {G4175), and has a root {G4176} meaning to be a citizen. So, as we have read, we are seated in *Heavenly places* and we are seated here in the physical realm. We have dual citizenships. We also are seated far above all powers and principalities, thus we can do as Jesus did while here on the earth, and walk in the earthly and spiritual realm at the same time. How do we do that? By simply keeping our mind's screen on Him. We can do our everyday, ordinary duties and stay conscious of His Presence. Which reminds me of Romans 12:1-2 MSG:

> So here's what I want you to do, *God helping you*: Take your everyday, ordinary life—your sleeping, eating, going-to-work, and walking-around life— and place it before God as an offering. Embracing what God does for you is the best thing you can do for him. Don't become so well-adjusted to your culture that you fit into it without even thinking. Instead, <u>fix your attention on God</u>. You'll be changed from the inside out. <u>Readily recognize</u>

what he wants from you, and <u>quickly respond</u> to it. Unlike the culture around you, always dragging you down to its level of immaturity, God brings the best out of you, develops well-formed maturity in you.

This verse tells us to *fix our attention on God*, to readily recognize what He wants, and to quickly respond. We can do this, as long as our conscience is clear. Sin separates us from God. Our sin not only separates us from Him, but also causes God to *hide His face* from us. Let's look at that verse in Isaiah 59:2:

> But your <u>iniquities have separated</u> you from your God; and your sins have **hidden His face from you**, so that He will not hear.

Did you know that our disobedience also sets us up for that barrier? We are hidden from God, because our heart and mind are not clean. If our conscience is not clean, we will not have access to Him, because we have separated ourselves from Him. We must keep sin out of our life by confessing it quickly. Don't let sin reign for weeks. The blood of Jesus Christ cleanses us from all unrighteousness (1John 1:9). Then our fellowship with Him is established again in both realms. Our conversation is in *Heaven* and our fellowship with each other is there also.

James 4:8 states, "Draw near to God and He will draw near to you. Cleanse your hands, you sinners; and purify your hearts, you double-minded." We want to remain in Him and we do this by keeping a clean conscience. As we stay in right standing with Him, even Jesus said we could be where He is and see His glory. Let's look at that verse in John 17:24 AMPC:

> Father, I desire that they also whom You have entrusted to Me [as Your gift to Me] may be with Me where I am, so that they may see My glory, which You have given Me [Your love gift to Me]; for You loved Me before the foundation of the world.

We have just learned that God's face will be hidden from us if we are in sin, but if we stay in right standing, we will even be with Jesus where He is, and see His glory. We will do this by focusing our mind on Him in *Heavenly places*, continuing to keep our mind on Him as we go about our daily duties. As I have said before, if we can master the ability to keep our mind on Him, then *entering into Heavenly places* will happen instantly. Our mind can be stayed on Him at all times, and our heart also, as it is purposely pointed towards Him. Then if we want to *enter into the Heavenly places*, we just close our eyes, and there He is, on our mind's screen!

As we close this chapter, I am believing that we have all come up higher in the process of *entering into Heavenly places*. We are keeping a clear conscience, and our minds are stayed on Him. The opening verse for this chapter speaks of the things which are not seen, are eternal. That word seen {G991} carries the meaning of: to see with the bodily eye, and to see with the mind's screen. Let's look at 2Corinthians 4:18:

> "while we do not look at the things which are *seen*, but at the things which are not *seen*. For the things which are *seen* are temporary, but the things which are not *seen* are eternal."

Again, to *enter into Heavenly places*, is much like diving or swimming under water. Once we *enter into Heavenly places*, at times we will have a different sense or feeling. There is a different way of hearing, and seeing. Our emotions will vary from moment to moment, as He speaks mysteries through us in the Spirit (1Cor 14:2). There's also an indescribable peace that's mentioned in Philippians 4:7 which states: "and the peace of God, which surpasses all understanding, will guard your hearts and minds through Christ Jesus." As we're in this realm, His peace is guarding our hearts and minds, which makes it easier to keep our minds on Him.

Let's pray:

> Holy Father, we do long to be in Your Presence. Help us to keep a clean conscience. Thank You that as our mind is stayed on You, You will keep us in perfect peace, so that we can e*nter into Heavenly Places*. We have learned that we are already seated with You in Christ Jesus, therefore we have access to You 24/7. We want to be *available* to You

to minister to others, and we dearly want to sit at Your feet and minister to You. Increase our ability to access our spiritual gifts. In the most magnificent name, Jesus. Amen.

Chapter 9

MEET WITH GOD

---

*And Moses brought the people out of the camp to **meet with God**, and they stood at the foot of the mountain.*

Exodus 19:17

We have finally made it to the chapter we've all been eagerly waiting for. The one chapter that we wanted to jump to from the beginning. I'm glad you waited and followed through with the other chapters, which were all building one upon another unto this point. From these chapters we have gathered that we must first have a *desire* for His Presence to even be able to *prepare our heart* and *a place for Him*. We know now that we must become a *bondservant* if we ever want to be *available* for Him to *knock* so that we may *enter into Heavenly places* to *meet with Him*.

First thing we need to remember here is that we live by trust and faith in the *Word* of God (2Cor 5:7). We have walked through the verses that encourage us to open the door by faith when He *knocks*. Let's look at Hebrews 11:6:

> But without faith *it is* impossible to please *Him,* for he who comes to God must believe that He is, and *that* He is a rewarder of those who diligently seek Him.

Again, Hebrews 11:6 plainly tells us that we can come to God. Is that what we just read or not? Then as we do this by faith, He rewards us as we diligently seek Him! From this verse we see just how important faith is, but how do we get faith? By simply hearing the *Word* of God (Rom 10:17). It's the washing of the *Word* of God that cleanses us, and that includes our minds from our thoughts and changes them to His thoughts which are His *Word* (Eph 5:26). Romans 12:2 states, "And do not be conformed to this world, but be transformed by the renewing of your mind, that you may prove what *is* that good and acceptable and perfect will of God."

His *Word* tells us that He keeps us in perfect peace as our mind or we could say, our imagination, is stayed on Him (Isa 26:3). Colossians 3:2 tells us to set our minds on things above. In the book of Revelation John was told, "Come up here," and instantly he was in the Spirit. John was on the earth, and yet in Heaven at the same time

(Rev 4:1-3). We too can experience such encounters with our Lord.

Before we go any deeper into how to *meet with God* (Ex 19:7), I need to clarify a few things. As previously stated, we can *meet with God* at any time or place by knowing the way. However, if we happen to be in a corporate prayer setting, then during this type of prayer we are always to follow the lead prayer (1Cor 14:40). The leader has heard from Heaven and has a plan or prayer strategy. Follow their lead, and do not allow yourself to get 'caught up,' unless the leader has otherwise specified. The next prayer setting is similar yet it's a petition of prayers in which we follow the prayer leader on a set of petitions that they have, and need us to be in agreement with (Matt 18:19). Again, do not allow yourself to get 'caught up,' unless otherwise specified by the prayer leader. Lastly, we have our own intercession that comes upon us, and we have our own prayer request, where we can freely get 'caught up,' and be led by Him (Rom 8:14, John16:13-15). All of these types of prayer are commanded and therefore good. The *Word* states that we are to always pray without ceasing (1Thess 5:17).

These types of prayers had to be addressed, because you must be warned that once you have entered into the Presence of God, all you will have to do is close your eyes and look unto Jesus, and you will be 'caught up.' We need to be aware of this, so that we can follow the prayer leader and stay decent and in order (1Cor 14:40). This has been very hard for me over the years, as I quickly get 'caught up,' by simply closing my eyes—looking unto Jesus—that I have had to train myself not to close my eyes, looking unto Jesus. Even with that, as we pray for extended length of times, I could easily just cross over by focusing on Jesus with my eyes open! My prayer for you is that you too will encounter His Presence in the same manner, learn from my mistakes and do accordingly.

Now, back to how to *MEET WITH GOD* (Ex 19:17), where we come either personally or with a group with or without a prayer agenda, and to minister unto Him. We have a great example in Moses, who talked to God face to face (Ex 33:11). When we research Moses, we find that he was faithful in all His house as a servant (Heb 3:5). He was faithful in building the tabernacle for God's Presence. Instead of that word faithful, we could say he was obedient in building the tabernacle of God's Presence. Obedience is better than sacrifice. Before we get to the tabernacle, let's see where God was telling Moses that He would first *meet with Him* in a thick cloud. We find this in Exodus 19:3-9:

> And Moses went up to God, and the Lord called to him from the mountain, saying, "Thus you shall say to the house of Jacob, and tell the children of Israel: 'You have seen what I did to the Egyptians, and how I bore you on eagles' wings and brought you to Myself. Now therefore, if you will indeed obey My voice and keep My covenant, then you

shall be a special treasure to Me above all people; for all the earth *is* Mine. And you shall be to Me a kingdom of priests and a holy nation.' These *are* the words which you shall speak to the children of Israel."

So Moses came and called for the elders of the people, and laid before them all these words which the Lord commanded him. Then all the people answered together and said, "All that the Lord has spoken we will do." So Moses brought back the words of the people to the Lord. And the Lord said to Moses, "Behold, I come to you in the thick cloud, that the people may hear when I speak with you, and believe you forever."

So Moses told the words of the people to the Lord.

I bring this up, because it wasn't long before the people who said, "All that the Lord has spoken we will do," was not followed through by the very next chapter. Exodus 20:19 states, "Then they said to Moses, 'You speak with us, and we will hear; but let not God speak with us, lest we die.'" They were afraid of the thick cloud which brought thundering and lighting with it. They were disobedient, and lost out on being in the very Presence of God. We do not want that to happen to us. Remember, we are to keep a clear conscious, a clean heart or mind's screen, and obey *His Word.* I'm reminded of a story in 1Chronicles where David was told how to build the temple of God, however, because he had blood on his hands, his son Solomon was the one to build it. In 1Chronicles 29:18 it states, "O Lord God of Abraham, Isaac, and Israel, our fathers, keep this forever in the intent of the thoughts of the heart of Your people, and fix their heart toward You." This verse is talking about how to build the temple. Let's look at that verse in the AMPC:

> O Lord, God of Abraham, Isaac, and Israel, our fathers, keep forever such purposes *and* thoughts in the minds of Your people, and direct *and* establish their hearts toward You.

This verse clearly states that they are asking God to keep the plans of the temple in their thoughts or on their mind's screen, and to direct their hearts towards Him. How neat is that? This prayer is helping them to stand, and be focused on how to build His temple, and keep their hearts toward Him. What a wonderful example of how to use our God given imagination. Remember what we focus on we connect with.

Let's once again go back to Ephesians 1:17-18 which states, "That the God of our Lord Jesus Christ, the Father of glory, may give to you the spirit of wisdom and revelation in the knowledge of Him, the eyes of your understanding being enlightened." The eyes of our understanding is where we get our imagination, and the word enlightened is where we get our English word, photograph. As we focus on Jesus to *meet with Him,* the anointing will come upon us and open the eyes of our imagination and begin forming a picture of what He is conveying to us. We're looking at things which are not seen with the natural eye, but with our mind's eye or screen. The *Word* states that Jesus is the image of the invisible God. Let's look at that verse in Colossians 1:15 AMPC:

> [Now] He is the exact likeness of the unseen God [the visible representation of the invisible]; He is the Firstborn of all creation.

From this verse we see that when we look unto Jesus, we are looking unto God. We use our mind as the vital link between the mind and the spirit. That's why the battle is in the mind. The brain is a great computer with infinite storage. We must renew it to the *Word* of God daily, and allow it to open the door when Jesus *knocks*. If we ever learn how to open the door to Jesus, then that will be stored in our brain, and we will have access to opening the door forever. That's why it's very important to be careful what we see, and hear, because it's stored and becomes part of us. You can't erase it. Therefore renewing our mind is a must.

Our spirit knows, hears, and moves with Him, but if our mind is not renewed, we will have a war between our spirit and our mind. Matthew 6:22-23 talks about if your eye be single, or in harmony with your spirit then your whole body is full of light and transformed. Then in Romans 12:2 we're told not to be conformed to this world but be transformed like the butterfly that is changed from being a creature that walks on the earth to one that can fly over the earth. We should learn to do the same.

The *Word* of God states that the words He speaks are spirit and life (John 6:63). When a rhema word or revelation comes, we feel it, it changes us. We then are encouraged to lay aside everything that is at enmity to the mind, and receive the engrafted or implanted *Word* with meekness which will save our soul which is our mind, will, and emotions (James 1:21). This rhema word becomes a part of us! The more we experience Him, the more our senses and feelings will be His. Take our body for instance, if we bump our knee, our body just knows the pain spontaneously, so will our spirit-man be exercised to sense or feel those promptings or checks by Him. All because we've renewed our minds with His revelation knowledge. In the spirit we want to be able to experience His Presence 24/7, but we'll never do that if we are relying on our outer shell of who we are to indicate to us what's happening in our spirit-man.

Hopefully we now can see how much we have to be obedient to, and maybe we can go on to what we do as we come to *meet with Him*. As I have emphasized before, it's very important to close our eyes. Even then for people who are easily distracted, it will be a challenge to keep their eyes closed. The question then is, who is most important, the people around us, or Jesus? The key is asking Holy Spirit to help us. We must first purpose in our hearts to *meet with God*; as we do, Holy Spirit will begin to help calm our minds. If our mind wanders, simply place it back on Jesus. The more we see Jesus on our mind's screen, the easier it will be to get 'caught up.' Focusing on Jesus, will bring Him to meet with us. We were made to *meet with Him*, and He loves our obedience in coming before Him. When we do, we are telling Him that He is most important to us, as we lay aside everything just to come *meet with Him*.

He will begin to show us things. We will have different feelings and our senses will be heightened. We may even smell odors like frankincense, myrrh, or cinnamon. As we become sensitive to Him knocking for us to come *meet with Him*, He may even show us parts of Heaven. We will know this by His description of what we are seeing as it lines up with the *Word* of God. We could possibly feel His tangible Presence as in a physical touch from Him. The more we set aside time to *meet with Him*, to just be with Him, the more He will open up the Heavens to us. Like when He told John to "come up here" in Revelations.

I have always kept a journal with me as I *meet with Him*. I use to keep my Bible with me, but now it's quicker to have my Bible on my silenced phone. I then can quickly look up something that He tells me, to see where it is in His *Word*. However, I only open my eyes when prompted, so that I can stay in that place with Him. He will also tell us things to come (John 16:13). You will know when you need to write it down. Just be aware that if you open your eyes you may find it hard to enter back in. This will lessen as you continue to encounter Him. As I have previously stated, all I have to do is close my eyes, or keep my eyes open and *focus on Jesus*, and I'm with Him. His Presence is overwhelming and powerful. You will experience a peace that truly does pass all understanding. Once you experience that, it will be hard to keep yourself from entering in every chance you get.

We can enter into His Presence, any place and any time. He is ever present to make Himself known to us, for He resides on the inside of us. We carry Him everywhere we go. The more conscious we are of His Presence, the easier it becomes to commune with Him. The more we encounter Him, the more people will recognize that we have been with Him. Oh, they may not say those words, but they will know that something is different about us. It's because of the Who that is on the inside of us is peeking through. We can't habitually be in His Presence with a one on one encounter and not have it shown on our countenance. We may not have to wear a veil like Moses, but our skin will have a glow. You know, you have seen people and just know something is different about them. You too will have the same said about you as you habitually *meet with God*.

As we come to the close of this book, I am so excited that you now have the tools of His *Word* to *meet with Him*. Without knowledge of His *Word*, we'll never make it to an encounter with Him. Everything He reveals to us will be in His *Word*. The more our love for Him and His *Word* increases, the more our *desire* to be with Him will also increase. Our *desire* for His Presence will cause us to *prepare our heart* and *a place for Him*. We will become a *bondservant* and want to be *available* for Him to *knock* at any time so that we may *enter into Heavenly places* to *meet with Him, any time* and *any place*. Eyes closed or eyes opened, as we focus on Him, He will meet with us!

Let's pray:

> Our Father in Heaven, thank You that You have made a way for us to come boldly to Your throne (Heb 4:16). Help us to keep a clean conscious and clear mind. We ask that You knock on our hearts more and more. Help us to be obedient to Your knock that we might meet with You (Ex 19:17). Our heart's desire is to encounter you in every way possible. May we fall deeper and deeper in love with You as You show Yourself to us. We do now purpose in our heart to prepare to meet with You. Enlighten our eyes to see the unseen. Help us to move with You in Heavenly places. In Jesus's name. Amen.

Conclusion

Here we are at the conclusion of, *Meet with God*. I am thankful that as you have read this book, you now have the knowledge of how to prepare yourself to *Meet with God*. We have learned that it is His will for us to come boldly before Him (Heb 4:16). He wants to meet with us even more than we want to *meet with Him* (Ex19:17). He created man to fellowship with Him (1Cor 1:9). If we follow these simple steps in each chapter, we can now get *'caught up'* at any moment we or He chooses (Heb 12:2). As we have built an even stronger relationship with the Trinity, we can see that we are actually walking together (2Cor 6:16). We belong to Him and He lives on the inside of us and we have total access to Him, and Him to us (John 14:23)!

If you read the Preface of this book, then you remember that the title of this book came by me literally hearing my pastor say the words, *"Meet with God."* That was supernatural, to say the least. This was the audible voice of God. I searched it out and found those *exact* words in

Exodus 19:17. Little did I know that it would produce a *Meet with God* team who seeks only His face. I want to remind you that during these meetings we actually saw that Shekinah glory of God in our sanctuary. Shekinah glory is the manifestation of the very Presence of God on the earth. This glory can manifest in a cloud by day or a fire by night (Ex 13:21), or a heaviness that caused the priest not to be able to stand and minister for the weight of His glory (2Chro 5:13). In 2Chronicles 5:13, the praises were going up before the Lord and caused His Presence to come down in the form of a cloud. That's the reason this small group got to actually see the glory of the Lord, because we were only there to minister to Him. We didn't have our own prayer request or agenda. We were only there to *meet with Him.*

Holy Spirit wants me to remind you of this manifested glory, because you too can experience Him in this manner. It doesn't have to be in your church, though I do pray that it will be seen in your sanctuary, however, this same glory can be seen wherever we are worshipping Him. God is Spirit and we must worship Him in spirit and in truth (John 4:24). He can show up in our *secret place*, and even outside as the cover of this book portrays. He has shown up in my very home many times, and each time had significance to His Presence. Seek Him while He may be found (Isa 55:6). Remember, don't always seek your own agenda, but simply come to sit at His feet as Mary did. The *Word* tells us that she had *chosen* the good thing, which shall not be taken from her (Luke

10:42). Let's purpose to choose to be *available* to Him and His Presence. As I have stated time and time again, there is nothing like His Presence!

I'd like to take this time to say, "Bless you," for your interest in this book, or more importantly, your interest in *meeting with God*. I know God has richly blessed your time spent being taught the simplicity of entering into His Presence. You now know that as you apply these steps you will always be able to look unto Jesus, the author and finisher of your faith, and see Him with your mind's screen (Heb 12:2). Once we have learned how to answer His knock, the door will always be open unto us (Rev 3:20). My heart's desire is that your heart's desire is to be able at any time to focus your affection towards Him, so that He will overwhelm you with His presence as He does me (2Chro 5:14). There is nothing in this world like a personal encounter with Him! And we can encounter Him through the steps listed in each chapter. We don't have to wait till we get to our church altar, or even to our *secret place*. He is a good, good Father who wants to communicate with His children through meeting with them (Ex 19:17). He can knock as we are –*"minding our own little business,"* as I like to say. We then have an opportunity to be *available* to Him, no matter what we are doing or where we are. The more obedient we are to be quick to answer His knock, the more available we become to Him, and He can then trust us to encounter Him in even greater ways. Let's purpose in our hearts to continually seek Him while He may be found (Isa 55:6).

For this prayer time, I want to pray personally for you! Receive this prayer:

> Father God, I am coming to You in *thanksgiving* for writing this book through me, so that others may experience meeting with You (Ex 19:17). I know that the heart and mind of the reader has been enlightened to Your ways of meeting with You. Thank You Father, that the reader knows Your *Word*, and has gained *desire* to *prepare their heart* and *a place* to meet with You. The reader has also learned that they must become a *bondservant* if they are ever going to be *available* to Your *knock* that they may *enter into Heavenly places* to meet with You. Father, continue to train them as they meet with You. May they experience You, as I have experienced You, and even in greater ways. Take them to *Heavenly places* as they look unto You. Thank You for over-whelming them with Your Presence as they set their affections upon You (Col 3:2). Father, I love You and I thank You for inspiring Your children to meet with You. In the name that we look unto, Jesus. Amen.

About the Author

Jennie Chapman and husband, Rusty, have a son which followed in his dad's steps and has now retired with 20 years in the USAF, married to a lovely wife, and raising two awesome children.

Jennie and Rusty are both ordained ministers. They were anointed by God to take up, Overcomers by Faith Ministry, in 1999, after the death of its founder, Amanda C. Davis. They have given away innumerable amounts of Biblical material, pray endlessly for the sick and hurting, are involved in missions trips to Dominican Republic, taught at their local Nursing Center, prayerfully accept speaking engagements, and preach with signs and wonders following. You can find more information at www.OvercomersByFaith.com.

You can also find more information about Jennie's books at www.JennieJChapman.com.

Author Website:

https://www.JennieJChapman.com

Ministry Website:

https://www.OvercomersByFaith.com

Home Church Covering:

https://www.LivingWord412.com

Social Media Ministry Page:

https://www.facebook.com/OvercomersByFaithMinistry

E-mail:

JennieChapman22@gmail.com

Books by
JENNIE J. CHAPMAN

Encounters with Him: Knowing That Still Small Voice

https://www.amazon.com/Encounters-Him-Knowing-Still-Small/dp/B0B7QPFXPV

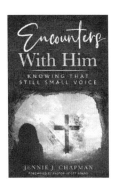

Overcomers by Faith Devotional/Journal: 100 Days of Seeking His Face

https://www.amazon.com/Overcomers-Faith-Devotional-Days-Seeking/dp/B0BJNBVKK8

8 Keys to a New Beginning: Building Relationship with the Holy Trinity

https://www.amazon.com/Keys-New-Beginning-Building-Relationship/dp/B0BN21JLLL

Simplicity in Hearing God Speak: Led by His Voice

https://www.amazon.com/Simplicity-Hearing-God-Speak-Voice/dp/B0D2VYKYBH

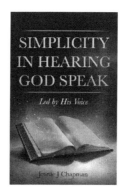

Free MP3 Downloads by
JENNIE J CHAPMAN

Free MP3 download Healing Scriptures
recited by Jennie J Chapman

https://www.dropbox.com/s/snku0ilsynshy9p/
Healing%20Scriptures.mp3?dl=0

Free MP3 download Precious Promises Scriptures
recited by Jennie J Chapman

https://www.dropbox.com/s/xc3mk87rnxug8im/
Precious%20Promises%20Scriptures%20-
%20Jennie%20Chapman%20-.mp3?dl=0

Donations Welcome:
QR Code

Or:
https://www.paypal.com/paypalme/obfm